22.00

International Textbooks in Art and Art Education

Consulting Editor

ITALO L. DE FRANCESCO

LITHOGRAPHY

Paysage des fleurs

Emil Weddige
"Paysage des Fleurs"
edition 30
25¾" x 19¾" (horizontal)

LITHOGRAPHY

by

Emil Weddige

INTERNATIONAL TEXTBOOK COMPANY

Scranton, Pennsylvania

PREFACE

Publication date is close at hand and the decision to write a book takes on new meaning and is now interwoven with experience. An experience vast and complex fraught with problems. It holds far greater significance than when this book was started over two years ago. Through the work there has developed a profound respect for people who write as part of their profession and repeat the task time and again. The whole team of persons who edit, set type, supervise, proof reproductions, and collectively guard intentions become as one and the result is the book. For a person like myself who is not a writer by profession and is not from experience knowledgeable of the multitude of problems involved, it is only due to blissful ignorance that books, such as this one, would ever be written because the bulk of problems other than writing might have altered the decision.

Artists and students who become interested in lithography are constantly exposed to problems and the assessment of values. We have answered countless letters and telephone calls regarding the subject. Sometimes a person, forgetting the time difference, has telephoned in the midde of the night to ask for help in preventing work from becoming coarse and dark during the pulling of the edition. On occasions I have talked by long distance telephone to students at another university with the conversation put through a public address system. We have received groups of students, who came by bus to visit my studio for an afternoon discussion. It seemed reasonable to write a book because no short discussion could be sufficiently complete. There is no thought on my part to eliminate or replace these various other ways of communication. A book is another broader means and has the important advantage of allowing continual reference.

The layout of this book has been planned to move from a general historic and philosophic viewpoint to specific problems. From the beginning of my experience with lithography a log has been kept of work in progress. This log was the instrument by which one could analyze the occurrence of problems and their solutions. Gradually a pattern of these happenings became apparent, and as the years went by there developed an understanding that became as a thread of relationships basic to all problems in the art of lithography. Art has to do with quality expressed through a form and from my viewpoint the particular form and the potential art are inseparable. Hence, it follows that it is not acceptable to make a small rough sketch and turn the sketch over to someone else and have them make it into a large painting or chisel a monumental piece of sculpture and then lay personal claim to the potential art. The same parallel is true in lithography. The total involvement with the stone and related materials are just as essentially a part of the art in lithography as applying paint to a canvas or forming materials in sculpture.

The artists represented have been carefully selected on the basis of the highest standards of quality. Each is an integral part of a broad cross section of countries, points of reference, and individual aesthetics. There are others who well might have been included if it had been possible to do so. One is faced with the problem of omitting significant contributors without desire or intention. Important workers in the area of lithography would certainly include Hans Hartung, Jean Le Moal, Marino Marini, Antonio Music, Rufino Tamayo, Richard Neal, Louis Hechenbleikner, Michael Ponce De Leon, Jack Perlmutter, John Muench, Jean Dubuffet, June Wayne, Hans Erni, Caroline Durieux, Marc Chagall, Karel Appel, Hans Trier, Pablo Picasso, Romas Viesulas, William Walmsley, and others both of the present and of the recent past.

The sections of problem analysis, specifications, and details, along with the approach to work, are intended to establish understanding toward evaluating and arriving at solutions. They are not to be considered as ends in themselves. It would be an error to interpret these as more than possibilities.

Time and again you will find me referring to basic conditions of temperature, age of materials, humidity, and the day to day changes that alter procedure and the effect of materials. It is appropriate to reflect here on an ancient anonymous saying, "one cannot put his foot in the same river twice." Change is constantly altering conditions in some way and one must be alert to take it into account. This suggests one of the most interesting aspects of writing a book because it must be basic to the aesthetics and problems and yet suggest to the serious student that there will always be new work to be done.

EMIL WEDDIGE

Ann Arbor, Michigan
September, 1965

ACKNOWLEDGMENTS

This book would not have been possible without the continual and inestimable encouragement and assistance of my wife, Juanita. Along the way many debts have been incurred, and grateful acknowledgment is made to students and associates. The people who have influenced the shaping of my point of view are numerous and share in my accomplishment. Persons like the philosopher O. O. Norris, artist Emil Ganso, artist Jean Paul Slusser, and associate Edward C. Pardon have given to me generously. I have received excellent collaboration on projects from numerous people, particularly Jacques Desjobert and Georges Pruvost. I wish to thank Miss Martha Dickenson, Weyhe Gallery; Albert Reese, Kennedy Gallery; Alice Lee Parker, Library of Congress; the Atelier of Edmond et Jacques Desjobert; Nichole Desjobert; Muriel C. Pardon; The University of Michigan, Horace H. Rackham Research Grant Committee; Robert L. Iglehart, Chairman, Art Department, The University of Michigan; to Dr. I. L. de Francesco for his excellent assistance in the editing of the manuscript; and to Kenneth R. Gromlich and John A. Wargo, whose dedication to quality and whose insight brought all aspects into focus. I express with gratitude the inspirational association with Alton Reeves, Vincent A. Hartgen, and Mack Stanley.

Acknowledgment is made to M. Myriam Prévot of Galerie de France for assistance and biographical material on Manessier, AAA Gallery, New York for loaning the works of Benton Spruance and Paul Wunderlich. All other works were loaned by the artists. Acknowledgment is also made to the Galerie Fricker for supplying biographical information on Jun Dobashi, and to Nordess Gallery, for biographical information on Ralston Crawford. Further acknowledgment is made to the following galleries: Forsythe Gallery, Ann Arbor, Michigan; Donald Morris Gallery; Detroit Artists Market; Arwin Gallery, Detroit, Michigan; Little Gallery, Birmingham, Michigan; AAA Gallery, New York; Kennedy Gallery, New York; I.F.A. Gallery, Washington, D.C.; the Felix Landau Gallery, Los Angeles, California; the Herbinet Galerie, Paris, France; and Ross-Talaley Gallery, New Haven, Connecticut.

The following photographers contributed:

Photographer	*Work Photographed*
Peggy Crawford	Ralston Crawford
Paul Castellon	Federico Castellon
Federico Castellon	Adolph Dehn
Photo Marc Vaux	Paul Aizpiri
Richard de Grab	Andre Planson
Interphoto	Massimo Campigli
Karin Szekessy	Paul Wunderlich
James Keson	Series on how to handle paper
Richard de Grab	Constantin Terechkovitch
Galerie de France	Manessier
Roger Hauert	Singier
Gene Fenn	Paris exhibition
E. C. Pardon III	Various interior views of the Ann Arbor studio
Sara Schwartz	Emil Weddige portrait
Marvin Silver	Garo Antreasian
Cecil C. Turner of Detroit Edison's *Graphic Arts*	Artist at work

EMIL WEDDIGE

CONTENTS

LIST OF LITHOGRAPHS

To
Edmond Desjobert
and
Juanita

EMIL WEDDIGE

Emil Weddige was born in Ontario, Canada, of American parents, in 1907. His early art training was in schools in the United States, and he received a Bachelor of Science degree from Eastern Michigan University and a Master of Design degree from The University of Michigan. Later he spent several years in advanced study and research in France. In 1937 he received a Fellowship at The University of Michigan, where he has remained and is now a professor in the Department of Art.

Weddige began exhibiting in 1934, and a painting, "Pip," oil on canvas 28" x 36", was awarded a first prize in a Michigan artists exhibition. In the following years his oils and watercolors have received seventeen prizes and awards. He maintains that it was shortly after he first experienced lithography that a pattern of form and intent became evident in his work. Since 1955 a greatly accelerated attention has been devoted to lithography.

He has lectured extensively and has been instrumental in establishing community art programs. He was elected by Michigan artists as a delegate to the national art conference in Chicago in the early thirties, out of which developed the Artists Equity. He is a founder-member of the Michigan Watercolor Society and served as its first president. In 1951 he organized the Michigan Printmakers Society. As a hobby he has been active in conservation and is a past president, of five terms of office, of the local chapter of the Izaak Walton League of America.

Numerous major commissions have been completed, including some for the Detroit Edison Company, Parke Davis and Company, and the Chrysler Automobile Company. Weddige was commissioned by the Dow Chemical Company to create a series of four full color lithographs depicting the major historical developments in paper. This was the largest commission done for industry in stone lithography printed by hand. In 1962 Weddige received a Tamarind Fellowship and also during that year spent several months of research and work in Spain, made possible by a Horace H. Rackham Grant from The University of Michigan.

Weddige pioneered in the contemporary renaissance of color lithography and has made a significant contribution to its development in America. His work enjoys the widening scope of an international audience and is known wherever graphics are shown through one-man and group exhibitions. The art world has honored his work in lithography with numerous awards and prizes. His work is in private and museum collections.

Emil Weddige

Emil Weddige
"Fisherman"
edition 35
13″ x 19¾″ (vertical)

LITHOGRAPHY

INTRODUCTION

The medium of lithography is a complex technical subject, and to work in the area one needs a critical attitude and precise working information. The purpose of this book is to help make the medium understandable and usable for students and artists many of whom will play an important role as educators in the future. In this respect The University of Michigan, Department of Art, has developed a significant number of artists in the area of lithography who are making an impressive teaching contribution in colleges and universities.

Lithography is not an end in itself. It is only one of the means of approaching art, and the substance of expression is no more complex than the society out of which it grows. Each conversely is largely the product of the other. This is not to state that art could produce society, any more than it would be possible for a song to produce a singer or paint, an artist. Art is produced by people for people, and the aesthetics of it as a major environmental factor continuously shapes qualities and reflects the critical standards of society. There are a few in each generation who constantly push the frontier of concepts to new horizons. This is as it should be; otherwise, our aesthetic environment and judgments would still be governed by the concepts of the past.

Things do change, and one cannot stand still and pretend things are not happening all around in every area simultaneously. With the passage of time, only the highest and most critical qualities of aesthetics persist as shaping factors for the developing present moment in time. One basic characteristic of all substance is change, and the moment change stops the substance ceases to exist, and its form immediately alters to a new form or disappears. Of all life man alone can direct and choose the kind of change that is to take place. Regardless of any other factors or excuses, man or society collectively is responsible for the kind of aesthetics, or in total, the kind of environment that exists.

It is well to keep in mind that change does not mean that the movement toward a new concept is necessarily for the better or that it is a matter of progress. It merely indicates that the person or the society is alive to new factors and is working. The appositeness of concept in relation to the total stimulus compounded collectively may and usually does produce symbols that are aesthetic landmarks. Contemporary society is constantly in the midst of a multitude of changing factors. Without the time-space factor, it is not possible to be very accurate in appraising aesthetics that are close with any high degree of accuracy. Occasionally one encounters an individual who assumes an inside type of mystical knowledge of all answers. This is rare, and the person is seldom very well informed nor is his opinion reliable. Critics, as a rule, are generally very conscious of the deep responsibility they exercise in the life of an artist, as well as with the public. There is not just one point of view, or one approach to aesthetics; there are many, and it is fundamentally essential that artists have freedom of choice and action. This does not mean freedom from responsibility, or license. Freedom is something that is earned through discipline, with the acceptance of responsibility toward the control of tools, materials, and concepts. The very desire or acceptance of such freedom makes it mandatory that all other artists are assured of the same right. It is only natural then that there will be many points of view. It does not follow that any are more right or less right; it merely indicates that there are differences.

With the preceding as a brief frame of reference, we can discuss some of the aspects upon which art criticism and art structure are based. To function as an artist, there are a few items and characteristics that are basic. These aspects are not dependent on training or the length of time of participation. It is possible to perform at a high critical standard without formal study or years of practice. This is not to deny that the great majority of developing artists would not need and profit by study and experience. The observation is made to clear the way so that it may be stated that neither study nor experience is the criterion by which we can either produce a work of art or be acclaimed as an artist. Some people study or paint for years with a closed mind, continuously rejecting the wonder and vitality of being alive to what is everywhere around them. Although there are exceptions, in the final analysis there does not seem generally to be any substitute for study and experience.

Art structure has to do with *form, content,* and *significance.* The period of formal study should include a critical understanding and performance grasp of each facet of the stuff out of which art is made. Likewise, art analysis or criticism is based on these same considerations. Of the three divisions, the artist is principally concerned with *form* and *content*. *Significance* is of very little working concern to artists. This aspect has to do with a comparable analysis of a number of works of one artist, or between one artist and another, or between several artists. Simply stated, *form* is the structural emphasis of a work of art. This is based on the elements of line, plane, mass, volume, light, texture, and color. These elements by natural affinity are selected by the artist for inclusion, exclusion, or emphasis. The relating of this natural selection to size, shape, position, and direction, when merged with concept, develops into a statement of *form*.

Content is the degree or type of emphasis for visual or sensory communication. These two aspects are very closely aligned to each other. It is possible to have an aesthetic quality of *form* with nonobjective *content*, but it is not possible to have an aesthetic quality of objective *content* without *form*. On this fact there is an amount of confusion, on the part of some. However, it is not new as a concept; actually, it is as old as art itself. The recognition of figurative or objective *content* is not the basic criterion for criticism or evaluation of a work of art.

For example, suppose we examine the paintings of nudes by Chagall, Picasso, Modigliani, Léger, and Kokoschka. In each instance the *content* is recognizable, and all the works are figurative to a degree. Is one to conclude then in these instances that because of the female nude these are fine paintings? It would be an incredible and unthinkable conclusion. The recognition of figurativeness, or, as it is generally referred to, "subject," has an infinitesimally small amount of importance, if any, in a work of art. At most, figurative *content*, when used, is merely that on which *form* is draped, so to speak. It is by *form* that one recognizes the works of Chagall, Picasso, Modigliani, Léger, Kokoschka, or anyone else.

The particular staccato texture of color in volume and light is Kokoschka, no matter what the *content*. Likewise, the two-dimensional planes, supported by receding and advancing juxtaposition of color with a ribbon of line, is Léger. An entirely different selection of artists could have been made such as Afro, Singier, Manessier, or Zao Wou-Ki. The work of these artists is, by contrast, abstract to the point of nonobjectivity. They are recognized by all standards of art criticism as great artists. Since these works are without easily recognizable figurative *content*, evaluation is based on *form*, without any loss to any other selection.

The recognition of the characteristics of *form, content* and *significance* is essential, but they are not the source from which the work of an artist begins. They are the outward substances for analysis and criticism. They are the things for systematic study in schools and universities. They are not the inner moving forces that go beyond the realm of objective description, and this is precisely why art is so difficult to attempt to teach or to understand. We know that there are types of reactions that encompass total sensory perception and that these complex reactions are not merely a response of reason from the brain. Responses of this type are referred to collectively as aesthetic reactions. They cannot be broken down into equations or for that matter very adequately described in words. Here we become involved with two areas of concern regarding art and the nature of man, namely, a relationship of illusion and reality which are constantly merging to produce these aesthetic reactions. Man seeks an inner and outer balance of the forces of his nature and his environment and rejects in many ways anything that disrupts the equilibrium. Generally speaking, we are slow to change. However, changing environment alters the conditioning factors, and consequently reality is constantly in a state of transition.

The first half of the twentieth century gradually conditioned people to expect everything to be provided in a predigested and scientifically-prepared capsule. The large mass mores or patterns of behavior that develop from the environment act as molders to conformity. As shaping forces they build a tremendous momentum and develop over a complete range from ordinary commercially biased points of view; for example, in regard to the fashion or style of clothes, there are few who are willing to break the pattern or mode of the day. This is even more true in the significant happenings of the time. In the same respect, consider the public reluctance to act or go counter to the accepted pattern of anything that can be named. At a given time, the majority will either have, want, or will be going after whatever is then popular. Not only that, but the group will to some extent exact a penalty from those who do not at that moment join and conform to whatever is the established pattern.

In spite of these powerful conditioning factors, there are always those within each generation who are fomenting change. A short while ago a young group rebelled against a mass of superficiality and the philosophy of doom, and they became known as Beatniks. This youth movement spread throughout the entire world within a relatively short period of time. A few years later we have now what high fashion terms that "casual look." This parallel could be made to cover practically every form and type of both behavior and the things that man uses in his society. Suffice it to state here that each and every important change from a historical point of record has been subject, first, to a period of condemnation, then a dormant period of acceptance, followed by a period of newly-established pattern. Reconsider the acceptance at the time of Leonardo da Vinci of the painting of the "Last Supper," or Rembrandt and the "Night Watch," or any of the later paintings of Jackson Pollack.

Man has the unhappy faculty of squabbling a great deal over minutiae of details, and many times loses sight of important issues. This is not to say that everything is good from one point of view or bad from another, but it is to state that man must learn eventually to allow complete freedom without any restriction except that required by responsibility and respect to every other man. In essence, to achieve this goal, it is mandatory that a great and dedicated renaissance of education take place.

It may seem that this discussion has gone far afield from art and aesthetic reaction, but the basis of each is also the structure of the other, and both determine the illusion and reality of the time. What is accepted as reality is so colored by what is brought to it by the individual that it is no wonder that there are so many diversified and contrasting points of view. The word "illusion" to be sure is used with some reservation and pertains to complex apperceptive inner-conditioned relationships that in themselves give meaning and qualities to symbols. These symbols in reality are not necessary for anyone else, nor can their probable existence be demonstrated in the object. However, this does not deny that these qualities that become more important than outward realities of substance are not perhaps the more real, even though their realities are the symbolic imagery and sensory intuitive concepts of the individual and not the object. Who knows the perceptive and responsive qualities of those persons who inhabit a particular home? To a large majority or even to anyone else that particular house in which they dwell may appear to be only a weather-beaten, run-down, and rambling shambles. The questions of inner relationship are the realities, however, and not what the outsider is able to see. How one reacts to the painting or to the poem or to the symphony is the reality of that moment for that individual. Does anyone take the position that the house is merely a beaten-up, run-down shambles of a structure and that the qualities from within are only figments of the imagination and do not exist? Is the reality of Crane's writing "rip-tooth of the skies torch acetelyn"[1] merely words? What is the reality of the painting, "La Femme," by Marc Chagall? Is the painting or the poem the symbolic reality for the conscience of those inner feelings—thoughts to our inner feelings—thoughts? No one questions that there are these myriad of relationships, and it would be impossible that they should be the same with all people. There is, however, a thread of universality, sometimes deeply hidden, in all significant things which basically moves through a form of aesthetics. This is equally true in art, as it is in all other things. These responses simultaneously cover time and space. Important art has produced for centuries the same comparable reactions in a complete cross section of people of all races, religions, and nationalities.

[1] Hart Crane, "To a Brooklyn Bridge."

The second half of the twentieth century has already seen important changes taking place in the point of view of scientific mechanization. Great universities, like Massachusetts Institute of Technology, whose specialty is technical scientific training, have completely revised their course structure to encompass within their basic curricula training in the imaginative and creative development of art in order to achieve the humanization of their programs. There are numerous indications that the emphasis is shifting from a mechanistic materialism to humanism and that man will learn how to utilize the freedom that he has earned through his centuries of struggle.

Art is a way of life, for the artist as well as the viewer; it is not merely an academic equation which is studied and added up. Only after one is free, in a sense, can aesthetic values be experienced. In this relationship, there develops a deep sense of awareness, rich in value, and a responsibility and love for the language of vision that gives meaning to all things.

1

THE BEGINNING OF LITHOGRAPHY

WITH the invention and discovery of lithography by Alois Senefelder in Bavaria, the fourth in the print mediums came into existence. Senefelder began his investigations in 1796 and completed them in 1811, and he named the new medium lithography.

He was the son of a court actor, Peter Senefelder, who performed primarily in Munich. Although the son was encouraged in literature and music, he was not encouraged in acting. It was natural, however, that Alois Senefelder, as a child growing up in a theatrical family, would have a strong leaning toward the written and spoken word in literature as it related to acting. This is pointed out primarily to indicate the difference in literature as read for individual consumption and as used during a shorter span by more people at a given time as it relates to acting or to music. It is important to mention the script for acting and the score for music because they were the fundamental stimuli in the eventual discovery and invention of stone lithography by Alois Senefelder.

About the year 1796, when Senefelder was a young man, an important event took place. He was encouraged to write a children's play, and on its successful completion it became necessary to furnish the cast with copies of the script. Printing was very expensive and could not be afforded. Senefelder considered printing the script himself on a hand press by cutting individual letters out of wood. When he found that this was not possible because of the time involved, he resorted to a method which is still practiced today, that of finding a sponsor.

The experience of writing the play and the difficulty in having it printed caused him to renew his efforts to find an easy and inexpensive means of reproducing the written word. Little did he consider at that time the possibility of illustration or art, as artists are concerned with his invention today. During this period he did a wide range of experimenting with existing forms of printmaking, namely, stencil, wood-block, and metal-plate. He was familiar with these methods of printing from working periodically in a small music publishing house. The latter part of his experiments revolved around the use of copper and zinc in an attempt to find a method of applying wax directly, or, as it is known today, a type of resist process. This did not succeed, but during these experiments he acquired a new stone slab such as an etcher uses as an ink slab to grind ink on. This ink slab was in common use and was called a Kellheim limestone. Although Senefelder had been working with metal plate and had used stone as an ink slab before, with the new ungreased stone he noticed for the first time that stains were left on the stone and that these stains could be removed and then replaced. At this early point he certainly was not involved in the chemistry of the materials but merely in the effect or appearance which ordinary tools and materials, previously used on metal plate, had on the appearance of the limestone. His curiosity was aroused, and he devoted more time to the stone, but he felt that the stone was too thin to be used in existing presses because of the possibility of breaking or crumbling. On further investigation he learned that limestone could be obtained in any thickness and degree of hardness desired. This now led him to further experimentation with the stone itself, and he put aside any further experimentation on copper and zinc.

The systematic discovery and invention of each aspect during about a fifteen year period certainly leads to the conclusion that the invention of lithography was no accident or mere chance of fate, as is sometimes indicated. It was well that these questions were fermenting in the mind of a creative genius of the stature of Alois Senefelder; otherwise, in lesser hands the invention of lithography would have been retarded for a number of years. The difficulties can only be alluded to in this treatment. One should keep in mind, however, that here was the discovery of a new print medium which achieved the desired end product but which had no relationship to known methods in other print mediums. It was necessary, therefore, to invent and discover the tools, materials, chemical properties and reactions, and to actually in some cases coin new words and names for things we commonly accept today. When we consider even briefly the magnitude of this research, followed by the almost immediate acceptance and use of the invention and discoveries throughout most of the world, and further that the findings of Senefelder have not been improved upon by other methods, materials, or equipment, then we are aware of the fullness of his contribution.

The new process of lithography became known in various countries of the world, and it eventually found its way to America in about the year 1820. Printing establishments located along the eastern coast in cities such as New York and Philadelphia began to use the process. Later companies farther west in Chicago, Cincinnati, and Detroit recognized the advantages of the new method. Stones were shipped from Germany at great expense. Some stones were quarried in the United States, but most of this stone was not of the proper hardness or consistency. Companies, such as Calvert in Detroit, Atlantic in Buffalo, Fusche and Lange and the company that bore the name of Senefelder in New York City, acquired a tremendous quantity of stone from central Europe. For example, Calvert, who printed on stone up to about the year 1920, had thousands of tons of stones stored in a library type of system, catalogued, referenced, and printed.

Although the participation of the United States in the art of lithography has been brief, it nonetheless has been distinguished. For the purpose here it is sufficient to go lightly into this background. Our early efforts were almost completely directed toward the commercial use of the medium. Since we did not have a tradition in lithography, many artisan-printers were imported from Europe, chiefly from Germany and France. A serious effort was made to train apprentices in the individual workshops in this country; however, the artisan-printer of the time guarded the intricate details of the medium very closely, to such an extent that the knowledge was apparently considered a professional secret and was not made available to the younger apprentices. Certainly the more apt workers were able to bridge this information gap, but indications are that development and subsequent advancement were slow. The many commercial books, texts, and essays of the time, show that information was lacking in detail at certain strategic points. Many students have said that it would be so much better to understand the medium before reading these texts, for then the texts could be filled in sufficiently to be understood in terms of the actual production of a lithograph. The attitude of professional secrecy toward the more intricate techniques within the process was one of the conditions that made the American role in lithography both unique and relatively short-lived.

The printing establishment of Currier and Ives made a lasting contribution to the art of lithography. The company worked in the East and sent its artists to various parts of the country to produce sketches for the editions that it pulled. Its most distinguished work was in the area of folk scenes and popular activities of the time. The series on the Mississippi landings, wharves, and ships, and the many that were done on the Western Movement, were not only a historic record of the time, but were also the beginning in the United States of the use of the medium as an art form.

After Currier and Ives the next most important landmark was the activity in lithography by a number of artists who were working in the United States just after the turn of the last century, or at about the time of the Armory Show in New York City. It would be impossible to list or attempt to list all of the distinguished artists who were in some way curious about the medium of lithography or who attempted to work in the medium. The possibilities of this period were perhaps the greatest of any time, either before or since. The American artist was awakening to the potential of lithography as an art form. The artists who tried the medium were able to find someone to help them in the printing of editions which were often quite small in size. Generally speaking, however, none of these artists were capable of completing the entire process on their own. They needed the collaboration of an artisan-printer with knowledge and equipment. At this time new inventions were being developed for the use of lithography in the commercial field which resulted in easier and less expensive methods.

It is indeed curious that at this period of transition artists in America began to seriously examine the medium of hand lithography as an art form. This examination was late because as quickly as the stone method of hand press lithography developed in the United States it also disappeared. Within a few years the large stacks of stones, the presses, and most important the artisan-printers and workers disappeared. What had been an operation requiring many persons—stone-cutter, stone grinder, pressman, artist, and printer, who had been involved in producing one piece of stone lithography—had disappeared, and an era was dead.

2

AMERICAN BACKGROUND

SINCE the twenties a number of important changes have taken place in the field of lithography. During this time printmaking exhibitions were very few and far between. A large majority of the public and those connected with museums, as well as a number of artists, looked on prints as a substitute for a drawing or painting form of art. There was a feeling that there was too much labor connected with printmaking, and, since it was in an edition of several pieces instead of one, it had a kind of diluted artistic quality. This type of negative reaction persisted for a long time. The print of that period was generally small or of the postage-stamp variety. It was collected more as a curio or as a substitute rather than as a fundamental art form, and the public in general took a very cool attitude toward prints.

This point of view is understandable when it is considered that the American public had been swamped during the previous two decades with poor reproductions and imitations from Europe that had been represented as originals. There had been literally thousands of brownish pseudo-art landscapes and French color reproductions imported and sold in America. There were only two possibilities for wall pictures for the general cross section of our people, either calendar reproductions or the equally questionable European reproductions. We did not have a genuine people's art, and the public had learned from their experience that they had been "taken in" on the so-called European print, which in most instances was not a print but a reproduction.

It should be made clear at this point, because it will be referred to again, that the word print as it refers to one of the four print mediums connotes an original art form that cannot be arrived at in any other way except through the particular medium itself. It is important that this definition be adhered to in order to avoid becoming immersed in the semantics of our language. It might have been better if the word "print" had not entered into the vocabulary of printmakers and this reference had been taken care of by the name of the medium. However, since it exists by use and tradition, it is necessary to deal with it. For instance, phrases such as "to print," as in printing letters, or "to print a reproduction" must be clearly distinguished from "pulling a lithographic print." The writer would like to recall this particular point at a later time in regard to authenticating and collecting.

During the period of transition there was a mere handful of artists in America who had acquired knowledge and skill in the handling of lithography. The most outstanding of these was Emil Ganso. His studio was completely equipped for work in the medium. His research developed the most critical level of skill, and the quality of his art extended the medium. At the untimely death of this creative artist, his art work in the medium was reaching new heights of beauty that were part of the foundations of the renaissance that has followed. The author had the privilege of knowing Emil Ganso and working in his studio. This was indeed a unique and rare opportunity for a young artist. Ganso was a great and exacting teacher; he knew the medium as few artists could know it. From him was acquired an insatiable thirst for understanding, a knowledge of lithography, and a hope for the development of potential skill. It was at this time that my first press was acquired and serious research in the medium was begun.

By the mid-thirties the door was almost closed on the possibility of obtaining fundamental and exact knowledge directly from people who had been trained commercially in the medium. When we consider that the commercial use of stone lithography had died within a relatively short period and that the printers had grown old during this same time and were not replaced, we can appreciate the fact that lithography was then almost a ghost medium. Equipment was becoming difficult to find because it was being sold for scrap iron or less. Stones were being hauled to lakes and pushed overboard. Toward the end of the thirties, the door toward the future of lithography had really been closed. It remained, as of that time, for the American artist to make the future of lithography what he would.

Various personal references are made only as a means of giving firsthand information about the conditions that all artists interested in lithography were facing. My work during this period, to about the year 1945, was extensive. A solid foundation had been acquired, but the solutions to certain problems were elusive. In connection with one of these problems, I traveled several hundred miles seeking the advice of a person described as an authority in printing. In terms of the present, the fee was the highest that could be paid for critical analyses. The information was given in guarded language, and the most pertinent details were held back. The one thing learned was that stale beer put in the washing solution would slow up the drying of the stone. The information, however, hardly seemed compensation for a month's salary. This experience resulted in a strong feeling of disgust toward the American practice of withholding information, and I decided to go to Europe for advanced work. After several years abroad there remained no doubt that the decision had been correct. My need for knowledge was both that of a serious artist in the medium and that of an educator.

Unlike the other three print mediums where printing is very routine because chemistry does not enter into the problem, lithography at the printing phase demands very exact information. In lithography the handling and subsequent printing of the stone are integral parts of the actual work on the stone, and cannot be separated from the artistic form of the final print. This is not mentioned as a negative inference to the other print mediums. It is merely to state a fact that one of the most essential characteristics of the medium of lithography is the chemical balance between all the material aspects. The printing in lithography is alive, so to speak, and constantly dependent upon the skill of the artist-printer. The work can be altered, damaged, or completely lost in the printing phase. Nothing is sure until the edition is completed.

A second aspect of lithography lies in the fact that if lithography is to exist for artists and to survive on the American scene, we must train artists to be their own printers. This takes time and incentive. This position is in direct contrast to the European procedure where an artist paints or draws on a stone and then turns the work over to a commercial artisan-printer for the edition. In any medium the basic characteristics of the medium fundamentally dictate the terms of the artwork or art form to some extent, and many times to a great extent. One cannot ignore the fact that a chisel is involved in a woodcut, any more than that a burin is involved in engraving. Likewise, lithography is concerned with certain characteristics which will be our major interest throughout this book.

It is interesting to look back at the exhibitions and catalogues of this early period. The character of the work gradually changed from a predominance of small genre type scenes. The print medium had the appearance of an apology to painting, and a print in any of the mediums that took on any type of new dimension in either size or art form seemed arrogant by contrast. However, the print was slowly altering and stretching existing concepts. A gradual and consistent change was taking place, although it is not possible to put a finger on any one aspect or development during these years. Each month and each new exhibition accounted for more changes. New exhibitions of prints were opening all over the country. By 1950, without being aware of it, we were in the midst of a renaissance of prints. Artists were feverishly active in producing prints. Color became a byword when mentioning the print medium. Because of the lack of knowledge and the desire to develop rapidly, many types of short cuts were taken in order to produce a color print, which requires much more knowledge and skill than the single plate, block, or stone.

Today we are at the highest point in the development of the print in America. Some of the most important exhibitions are devoted exclusively to prints. In the area of lithography we are at a time when it is necessary to re-evaluate and avoid making the same mistakes twice. The future of lithography for artists in America will be determined in the next ten-year period. In the writer's opinion, if we are to continue to produce lithography as an art form in the United States, we have the problem of stimulating and training the artist to be a total lithographer, not just a collaborator in the medium. To this goal I have devoted the last thirty years of my work as a teacher. This position is re-affirmed by students I have trained, who are now teaching in universities from Maine to California. Throughout the development of this particular period, other dedicated artists have been faced with the same frustrations and the need of solving the same problems. Collectively, the students trained in art schools and universities, who are now teaching, are the strength of the future of the medium. It is understandable that a student cannot within a very short period of time become as highly skilled and polished a printer as those in Europe, but he or she can become inspired with a desire for quality which will eventually produce the number of highly skilled people necessary to meet, at a critical level of quality, the needs of American art. Each year established painters and sculptors become interested in lithography. Their collaboration with an artist-lithographer is welcomed because the works produced extend the scope of the medium and add to its total stature and vitality as an art form. There is a handful of scattered studios in the United States where artists can work in the medium of lithography. The most unique and outstanding of these is the Tamarind Lithography Workshop. I was fortunate in being invited there as a Fellow, and the experience was excellent. The work and friendships formed with the staff and other artists will not be forgotten. The concept of the workshop by its director, June Wayne, is a vital bridge to the future of lithography for it offers mature artists in other areas an opportunity to become acquainted with the medium.

Although the contribution of the art form of lithography in America has been brief, it has been unique in its quality. This quality stems from the fact that we have had to "dig it out" for ourselves, and this gives it something which the European print often lacks. This does not mean to indicate that the European print at its best is not a great print. (This subject will be taken up later in detail.) It does indicate, however, that a difference in aesthetic quality is beginning to be manifested in the work of the younger American artists. The European artist has depended largely upon the commercial artisan-printer as a collaborator, whereas in America the artist has been attempting to be self-sufficient. Conversely, there has developed in America an attitude of self-reliance and of individuality which has become part of a structural attitude toward the medium as an art form.

3

THE EUROPEAN SCENE

THE European scene in lithography, in contrast to that of the United States, is completely different both in tradition and practice. Of course, there is every reason why it should be since lithography had its birthplace there. As has been mentioned, it was not long after the discovery and invention of lithography that a complete tradition was built up in each of the countries of western Europe. The most concentrated work, and, it might be added, also the most advanced, was in Germany, Austria, Belgium, and France. Because of migrations resulting from the two World Wars, France became the center of lithography with the most important standards and certainly the highest level of critical development. With the passing of the old city of Leipzig during World War II, it seemed that everyone in lithography of serious intent migrated to Paris. Undoubtedly there were other attractions, but there is absolutely no doubt that the ateliers in Paris, for example, those of Edmond Desjobert and Fernand Mourlot, represented the best of the thinking and tradition, not only of France, but, it would be safe to say, of the entire western part of Europe. These houses exemplified in every detail a mature vintage, so to speak, of the pinnacle of perfection in the art of printing by stone lithography and the highest form of collaboration that has ever been attained in the relationship between the artist and the artist-printer.

Somehow this brief mention of Edmond Desjobert, whom the author knew personally, seems inadequate. The simple facts do not fully convey the kind of relationship that is meant. Edmond Desjobert was not only one of the greatest printers of all time, but was also a wonderful and sympathetic person with insight and wisdom. He could feel with deep concern the problems of the artist and his struggles for individual expression. Edmond Desjobert lived and worked with *joie de vivre*, a wonderful and long life.[1] Thoughts of this remarkable person recall a statement made by Emil Ganso when he said, "A lithographic press is a demanding and wonderful thing, do not only see it but listen and it may speak. In the world there have been perhaps six great printers. Whoever can hear this press speak, may after a lifetime add to that number." To this inner circle certainly will be added the name of Desjobert. The distinguished tradition of the house of Desjobert will now be carried on by his son, Jacques Desjobert.

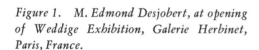
Figure 1.   M. Edmond Desjobert, at opening of Weddige Exhibition, Galerie Herbinet, Paris, France.

With this long and highly established pattern of printer and artisan relationship throughout Europe, there has been little or no need for the young developing artist to seek out the techniques and to develop the skills that are required to learn all phases of the medium of lithography. Some aspects were readymade for him and at his fingertips. Without preparation the young artist could step into a printing establishment and go to work. To be sure there was, and still exists, a complete range from ordinary to extraordinary printing establishments. Nonetheless, the point is that the young artist had no challenge to learn

[1] M. Edmond Desjobert died May 10, 1963 at the age of seventy-five.

Figure 2. Mme. and M. Jacques Desjobert.

the total medium. These establishments were a great asset to the developed artist-lithographer, but a great stumbling block to the inexperienced student. Perhaps this is the most important basic difference in practice between American and European lithography. With no challenge for the young developing artist to learn lithography as a complete medium, he accepted his limitations of half knowledge, and gradually over a period of years, most of the work of a generation of young artists has become less vital, more stereotyped, and more impersonal. It needs to be borne in mind that we are not discussing mature artists in this connection, artists such as Pablo Picasso, Marc Chagall, and Henri Matisse, to mention three, or any of those featured in this book. They were not hindered by the lithographic advantages of their environment. Each had learned the medium completely and was capable of the total performance.

This basic difference in procedure has been discussed for a long time, and I personally do not believe there is a single answer to the question. Perhaps there should not be one. It depends entirely upon the position taken, whether one is interested in educational goals or in arriving at what appears to be the highest quality of technical work in the shortest length of time. There is room for both points of view. Eventually young artists in Europe will be more concerned with putting the stamp of their individual points of view on the end product of the print. In order to do this they will have to know more about the medium. When this time comes, Europe will be in a dominant position of leadership.

On the other hand, we cannot transplant, as was attempted during the height of the commercial period, artisans to America and establish a tradition on the European basis. With the vast distances in America it would be false to hope that there could be as profuse a network of workshop studios as that found in Europe. If artisan-printer workshops are maintained in only a few scattered cities throughout the United States, then the great majority of students, young artists-to-be, and established artists will be out of touch with the main developments in standards of quality, and there will be little hope of being able to either maintain quality or develop lithography on a basis that would ensure its continuance in America. The point of view that has been in effect in America for approximately the past twenty years has been that students in our colleges and universities in the art of lithography should be trained in all phases of the

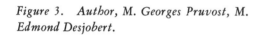

Figure 3. Author, M. Georges Pruvost, M. Edmond Desjobert.

medium. The places where lithography is being taught geographically cover the United States. With the training of the artist-student as a total lithographer and with the gradual diffusion of these students throughout the country, it should only be a generation or two before we are again in a position, from the standpoint of equipment and knowledge, to carry on a tradition in the art form of lithography. Essentially there are these two points of view and, as has been indicated, there is not a clear-cut answer as to which is better. It is hoped that during this time of development educators and people in positions of influence will be working in an unbiased way, with both points of view in mind, to achieve an American solution.

The lithographic prints of European artists are by all standards as fine in quality as those done anywhere. Some give leadership to the medium. In discussing European prints it is important to keep in mind that the writer excludes completely the works that are done in the print medium exclusively by the dealer and artisan-printer from paintings or sketches by any artist. This practice is a travesty on the medium and should be completely discouraged. It is not a relationship between artist and artist-printer to produce a print. It is instead a relationship of two persons removed from the artist, with the sole purpose of producing a piece of commercial merchandise for easy profit. This practice is a mockery of all standards of education, art, and ethics. No work is an original print of a particular artist unless the artist does the actual work on the stone or plate. The line is drawn at this point and no amount of discussion or coercion can change the point of view. It is disgusting and revolting to see the large number of works that are released to the public under misrepresentation and falsification. The practice usually involves the work of the older and most highly established European artists, generally those who have recently died. It is not easy to understand why it is allowed. It does not seem possible that any living artists allow it, and yet some subscribe to it. It appears that an over-zealous art market place is largely responsible. To present this issue and not to document it is unfair to the reader. However, it is understandable that the author has no desire to become entangled in lawsuits. On the other hand, personal integrity would not allow this question to pass unmentioned with the pretense that it does not exist. Some suggestions are made in the chapter on the Collector and Artist.

Our concern regarding the European printmaker is with the positive aspects of quality, and of these we have many. Artists, such as those whose works are reproduced in this book, along with a few others, have broadened and extended the medium in scale and aesthetic content.

Physical size in itself is not important nor does it give importance to a work. It does have impact and is like a comparison between the mouse and the elephant. The elephant is less apt to go unnoticed. The mouse in the cookie jar, however, is large in scale and will be seen; whereas the elephant in the kitchen, even a large kitchen, would be ridiculous. What we are concerned with is not just physical size but scale in relation to tools and concept. An engraving by Albrecht Dürer, although physically very small, is monumental in scale and concept. The tools and aesthetics are in harmony. A physically large print produced with the same tools would, as the size increased, become inappropriate to express the concept. Largeness, with a relationship of beautiful scale, is an important characteristic of the work of the contemporary scene. Psychologically this may have its roots in the vastly increased space concepts of science and its new horizons.

Technically and aesthetically, at its best the European print is elegant. In the hands of our modern masters, the contemporary European print is the best that has been produced in the history of printmaking.

Along with changes in the scale of prints, there has been in recent years a strong movement away from other art mediums, and consequently the lithographic print is more functionally itself. Techniques developed out of the characteristic peculiarities of the medium are emphasized. Color is used not as an adjunct to black but as an integral part of the compositional concept. Eventually this discussion can lead only to a consideration of art form, because no amount of technical skill can cover shortcomings in this regard. Here the lines are tightly drawn between the work of the American and European artist. It is believed that in terms of structure, content, and significance the two areas, when viewed at their best, are about equal.

4

ARTISTS AND THEIR WORK

CLINTON ADAMS

Clinton Adams was born in Glendale, California, in 1918. He studied at the University of California at Los Angeles where he received a Master of Arts degree in 1942. In 1948 he was introduced to lithography through working with Lynton R. Kistler, a master printer in Los Angeles. The career of Clinton Adams has beeen equally distinguished as an artist and an educator. He served on the faculty of UCLA from 1946 through 1954, teaching painting and later lithography. He has been Chairman of the Department of Art at the University of Kentucky and at the University of Florida. At present he is Dean of the College of Fine Arts at the University of New Mexico. He has also served as Associate Director of the Tamarind Lithography Workshop.

The artwork of Clinton Adams is well known through numerous one-man exhibitions both here and abroad. His lithographs are on exhibit in the most notable museums, including the Art Institute of Chicago, the Museum of Modern Art in New York, and the Victoria and Albert Museum of London. The aesthetics of his art develop from a content which seems nonobjective. The overall structure of his work is in the classic manner of pure planes in space, often enriched with a formal use of texture. The effect of his work is quiet, with a quality of monumentality.

Clinton Adams
Artist's proof
15" x 18¼" (vertical)

PAUL AIZPIRI

Paul Aizpiri was born in Paris on the 14th of May, 1919. His father, the sculptor, Ignacio Gorriti de Aizpiri, enriched his life from the beginning with the wonder of art. However, because the life of an artist was so difficult, the father persuaded young Paul to seek a trade. In spite of years spent as a cabinetmaker and cleaner of old paintings, the artist in Paul won out with slow certainty, but not without a great struggle. During the war Aizpiri was made a prisoner in Brittany but later escaped, only to return to the prison of occupied Paris. Although, when time permitted, he was very active in painting, it was not really until 1950 that he was able to devote his full time to painting.

His works completed since that time have been staggering in number, and his stature as an outstanding creative artist of his day in painting and lithography has been assured. Nature, through people and landscapes, is his main source of content; while his structural form develops out of an intricate labyrinth of angles and prisms of spacial color. The work in lithography by Aizpiri has been profound, and he brings to the medium, in works such as "Le Cid," a depth of feeling for life and the magic of the things of nature. The art of Paul Aizpiri is known in museums throughout the world.

Paul Aizpiri
Artist's proof
"Musicians"
30" x 22¼" (horizontal)

GARO Z. ANTRESASIAN

Garo Z. Antresasian was born in the year 1922 in Indianapolis, Indiana. His formal study was at the John Herron School of Art, where he received a Bachelor of Arts degree. From 1949 to 1950 he worked as a Mary Milliken Fellow. His advanced study in printmaking included work in New York with Stanley William Hayter and Will Barnet. He is at present an instructor of advanced painting and lithography at the John Herron School of Art. Antresasian is a notable American artist whose work has been primarily in painting and printmaking. He has completed several mural commissions. One of the most distinguished is housed at the University of Indiana.

Garo Antresasian has brought great zest to the medium of lithography where in recent years he has made a contribution of the highest order. His color lithographs have been extensively exhibited throughout the United States and are a part of the permanent collections of numerous museums and private collectors. His work in lithography is conceived in the total use of the medium. It is rich and full in form, and there is a merging of all aspects to attest to his understanding and mastery of this art.

Garo Z. Antresasian
Untitled
6/14 edition
25" x 33¾" (vertical)

9 /hulucsican '62

MASSIMO CAMPIGLI

Massimo Campigli was born in Florence, Italy, in the year 1895. Since 1919 he has lived most of the time in Paris. He also works in Milan, Venice, and Rome. Gradually since his first arrival in the art world of Paris, Campigli has abandoned all early connections with the theories for the vogue of the day. However, one area continues to hold a strong fascination for him—the museums of the ancient arts. Campigli sums up a major premise of himself and his work when he states, "I am a man with the most accommodation in the world for the things that do not have extreme importance; I am understanding or indifferent; but for the things that count in life, like painting or for example a great love, I have the most determined will and the most obstinacy that it is possible to imagine."

He is an extremely prolific and hard working artist. He would willingly give up all things except his indispensable regard for work and for woman. Within my knowledge, the female form appears without exception in his work. It is a richly-endowed form, overflowing with every attribute of feminine beauty and loveliness. Throughout his distinguished career, Campigli has received the most coveted honors that the world of art can bestow. His work touches with beauty and understanding every age, country, and language.

Massimo Campigli
Proof of the artist
22 1/4" x 30" (vertical)

I.G.   CAMPIGLI 62

FEDERICO CASTELLON

Federico Castellon is an American artist who was born in Almería, Spain, in 1914. His first view of the United States was as a young student in 1921. He was granted a four-year Fellowship by the Spanish Republic in 1934 and worked in Paris, France, for about two and a half years. He then returned to the United States where he took up residence. He was awarded a Guggenheim Fellowship in 1940, followed in 1949 by a grant from the National Institute of Arts and Letters and in 1950 by a second Guggenheim Fellowship. In 1955, Federico Castellon was a member of the United States Cultural Exchange Program and lectured in South America.

The work of Castellon has been honored throughout the art world, and he has received numerous awards and prizes, including the Logan Prize of the Chicago Art Institute, the Eyre Medal of the Pennsylvania Academy of Art, and a first prize at the Library of Congress. His work is known by an international audience and has been viewed in over 35 one-man exhibitions and group shows. Federico Castellon brings to the art of lithography a depth of feeling and a mastery of the medium seldom reached in any art form.

Federico Castellon
"The End of Dreams"
10/40 edition
19¾" x 25¾" (vertical)

42

ANTONI CLAVÉ

Antoni Clavé was born in 1913 in Barcelona, Spain, one of the richest creative environments of our time. He studied as a young student at the School of Beaux Arts of Barcelona. Like many other Spanish artists, he migrated to France, and in 1939 he had his first exhibition at Perpignan. As a person he brought to Paris the verve and magic spirit of the pure Catalans. The works of Edouard Vuillard, Pierre Bonnard, and Chaim Soutine, which he was seeing in depth for the first time, affected him greatly. During his formulative years, he turned to many means of expression, such as the theater, book illustrations, and posters. These avenues helped make possible his great interest in research in painting and lithography.

His work includes lithographs in black and white for Voltaire's *Candide,* 1948, and the set decorations for the Roland Petit Ballet of "Carmen" in 1949. Important illustrations were done in 1950 for *Gargantua* by Rabelais, followed by extensive lithography and painting to the year 1956. From 1957, as the progress of his work unfolded, Clavé went from painting to tapestry, to bas-relief, and to sculpture. Throughout all of these periods of research up to the present time, his work in lithography has been continuous and affected by each of his new experiences and has established him as one of the most distinguished artists of our time.

Antoni Clavé
Proof of the artist
30″ x 22¼″ (horizontal)

Claue

Épreuve d'artiste

RALSTON CRAWFORD

Ralston Crawford was born in 1906 in the city of Saint Catherine's, Ontario, Canada. His formal study was done at the Pennsylvania Academy of the Fine Arts in Philadelphia and the Barnes Foundation, Merion, Pennsylvania. He has traveled and worked extensively in the United States and Europe, especially in Spain. It can be said that he has never ceased his education, which is attested by his stature as an artist.

His work in painting and lithography is known internationally through 27 one-man exhibitions in painting and 17 one-man exhibitions of lithographs. Crawford's work is in the permanent collections of numerous museums and private collectors. It should be noted that he is a photographer of great talent. His photographs cover his travels and include a series on the birthplace of American Jazz. He has been invited as a visiting artist and lecturer to many American universities and is a gifted teacher. Outside of his work he has a great and searching interest in automobile racing.

Many forces have contributed to his development, all related to his basic activity of making pictures. The aesthetics of his art show that he is searching out the rapture of nature and environment; he seeks basic meanings, and his work distills his findings. On the world scene, the work of Ralston Crawford holds a position of honor among the best in contemporary art.

Ralston Crawford
Untitled
15″ x 22¼″ (vertical)

Ralston Crawford

ADOLPH DEHN

Adolph Dehn was born in midwest America, in Waterville, Minnesota, in 1895. As a small boy he began drawing, and at nine years of age a drawing of a train, shown at the local fair, attracted the praise of the town, and after that he was referred to as "the artist of Waterville." This indeed was an excellent gift of recognition, something of spiritual substance that a child could hold on to and from which to build and grow. Adolph Dehn from that time forward has never stopped reaching toward new horizons and, what is more, attaining them. He attended the Minneapolis Institute of Fine Arts and won a scholarship to the Art Students' League of New York City. Later, by dint of frugalness, Dehn continued his studies in Europe, where he lived in Vienna for four and a half years and frequented Paris, Berlin, London, and Rome.

As a painter and lithographer he is an artist of great distinction and worthy of the pinnacle of most critical praise. His lithographs are known internationally wherever prints are shown. Countless museums and private collections cherish his work. Important commissions have also been done, including work for the Standard Oil Company and the Book-of-the-Month Club, and a book on lithography. In the medium of stone lithography for artists, Adolph Dehn has been an American pioneer. The world of art has bestowed its most coveted laurels on this artist who has revealed the beauty of the things, the places, and the people with whom he has come into contact.

Adolph Dehn
"In the Night"
17¾" x 22" (vertical)

In the Night.   Adolf DEhn

JUN DOBASHI

Jun Dobashi was born in Tokyo, Japan, in 1910. In 1938 he completed his studies at the École des Beaux Arts in Tokyo and in that year visited Paris for the first time. Like artists throughout the world, the spell of Paris was too much, and Dobashi returned to France in 1953, where he has remained ever since. His first exhibition took place in Paris in 1954, and since that time he has been extremely active in the world of art. The work of Jun Dobashi belongs to the international foundations of symbolic nonfigurative art and aesthetics, to which he brings the flavor and mystery of the East.

He is a prolific worker, dividing his time between painting in oil, gouache, and lithography. His work bursts with color, and its content is basically concerned with the symbolism of inner nonhorizon space. In viewing his work one gets a certain indescribable awareness—as if there is a very personal and private conversation between the viewer and the work. His pictures have a compelling appeal to be understood through feeling. His work has been increasingly shown in exhibitions in many countries, including England, Japan, and Belgium, as well as the United States. Dobashi enjoys an ever-widening audience and increasing acclaim and honors.

Jun Dobashi
Untitled
Artist's proof
$19\frac{3}{4}''$ x $25\frac{3}{4}''$ (vertical)

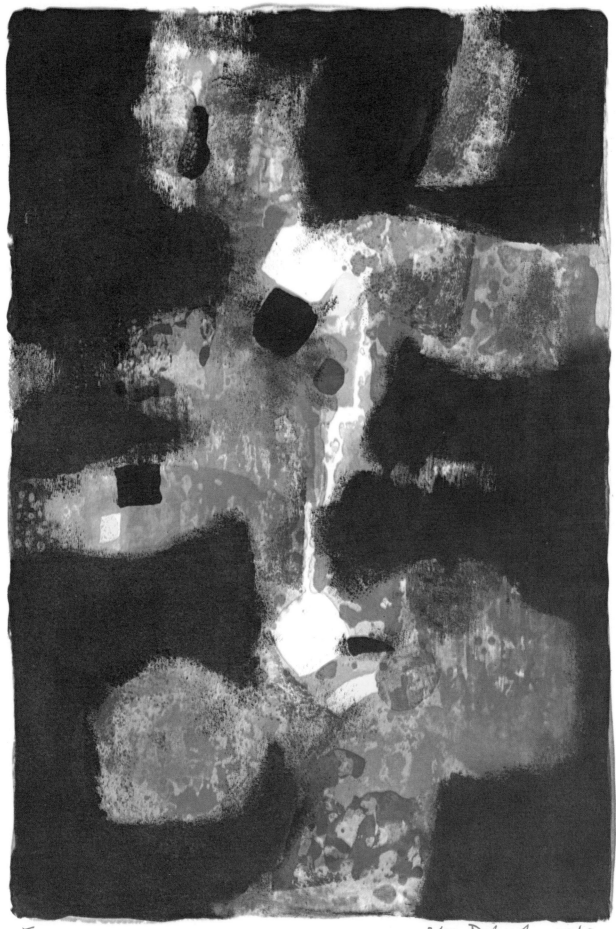

E.A   Jim Dobach 1962

ALFRED MANESSIER

Alfred Manessier was born on December 5, 1911, at Saint-Ouen. He is a French citizen. His childhood was spent at Abbeville, and he studied at the lycée and at the École des Beaux Arts of Amiens. Manessier moved to Paris in 1929, and for a short while he was a student of architecture. He spent a large amount of his leisure time visiting the Académies of Montparnasse and continuously frequented the Louvre where he became acquainted with Le Moal.

Manessier left Paris in 1936 and returned in 1938. These years were a critical period in his development. Several countries surrounding France, especially Switzerland, were becoming acquainted with his work, and important museums were adding their respects. The theme of religion and the relationship of form were maturing, particularly in the aspect of color enhanced by an intricate network of compositional planes. Rhythms established the basis of the overall harmony.

Gradually, over the recent years, his work has become more and more abstract and at the same time color has become increasingly dominant. Manessier is acclaimed by the entire world of art. He is a universal artist, and his art communicates on an international basis.

Alfred Manessier
Proof of the artist
39¼" x 29¾" (horizontal)

Épreuve d'artiste

Mauni~

ANDRÉ PLANSON

André Planson was born in 1898 at Ferté-sous-Jouarre, not far from Château-Thierry. His secondary studies were at the College of Meaux. He later moved to Paris where he lives and maintains a studio at the present time. His fondness for the French countryside frequently takes him to Brittany and into Provence, and over the years he has constantly returned to Ferté which to him is that corner of the earth where he feels completely at home and where his great talent is brought out to its fullest. The French government has on several occasions called on him for important commissions. Murals which he did for the Pavillon de France a l'Exposition in 1937 are now in the Musée d'Art Moderne, Paris. More recently notable contributions have been made to the theater Comédie Française and the Opéra Comique.

Planson is an artist who merges the most distinguished characteristics of the past with the universal language of contemporary art. In addition to his murals and paintings, his long career has been punctuated by his numerous illustrations of books. This distinguished artist carries with fitting nobleness many official citations, including Officier of Arts and Letters, Member of the Institute de France, and Chevalier de la Légion d'honneur.

André Planson
"Regates en Bretagne"
Artist's proof
25¾" x 19¾" (horizontal)

bw. Plamson

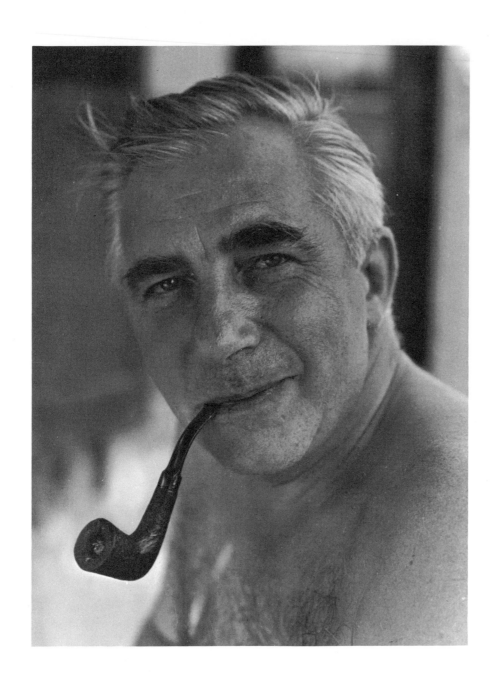

GUSTAVE SINGIER

Gustave Singier was born in 1907 in Warneton, West Flanders, Belgium. He is a naturalized French citizen and has lived in Paris since 1919. Singier began painting at the age of fourteen and later studied at the École Boulle. He began exhibiting regularly in Paris in 1936. Since that time, although a quiet and retiring person by nature, he has been a teacher at the Academy Ranson, the secretary of the Salon d'Automne, and was a founder member and at present a committee member of the new salon of young independent painters. Georges Charbonnier, in his book *Singier* states, "At not any moment of his life has Gustave Singier belonged to a group or of a tendency. He has never made an echo of a doctrine or a manifest." In view of this one might think of Singier as not effecting an impact on his environment and his time. Instead the brilliance of his work shines as clearly as the sun breaking through the cloud after a summer rain.

Painting and color lithography are the principal mediums through which he communicates. The structural form of his work has its foundation in semiflat two-dimensional color. There is a highly developed calligraphic juxtaposition of symbolic elements that punctuates his every attitude of content which has its departing point in nature. His work is coveted by all lovers of art.

Gustave Singier
Artist's proof
22 ¼″ x 30″ (vertical)

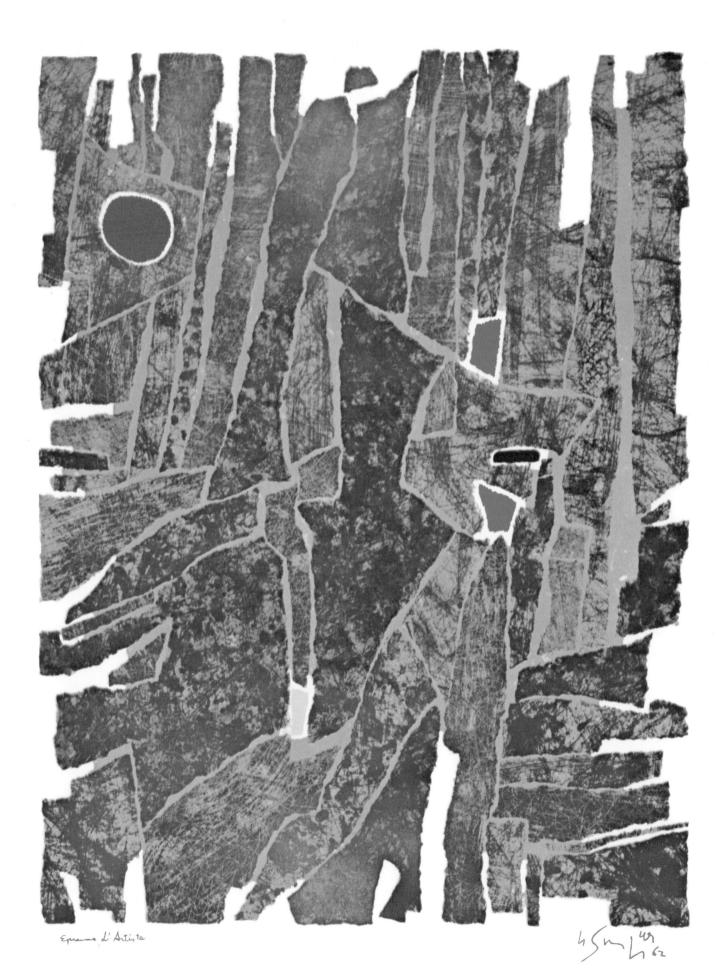

Epreuve d'Artiste

BENTON SPRUANCE

Benton Spruance was born in Philadelphia in 1904. He studied at the University of Pennsylvania School of Fine Arts and the Pennsylvania Academy of Fine Arts, where he was awarded two Cresson Traveling Scholarships in 1928 and in 1929. Beaver College awarded him an honorary Master of Arts degree in fine arts and in June, 1962, the Philadelphia Museum College conferred an honorary Doctor of Fine Arts degree upon him. His distinguished career as one of the foremost artists of our time has run parallel with his work in education as a teacher, and at present he is Chairman of the Fine Arts Department of Beaver College.

His work in painting and lithography has received the highest laurels that the art world can bestow, including two Guggenheim Fellowships, and in the past decade and a half it has received 20 first prizes. His work is in numerous private and in most public collections including the Museum of Modern Art, the Lessing J. Rosenwald Collection, and the Whitney Museum. The aesthetics involved have a quality of mystery and are rich in spiritual values. His work in lithography is honored wherever prints are known.

Benton Spruance
"Dark Bed"
ed./28 edition
33¼" x 25" (horizontal)

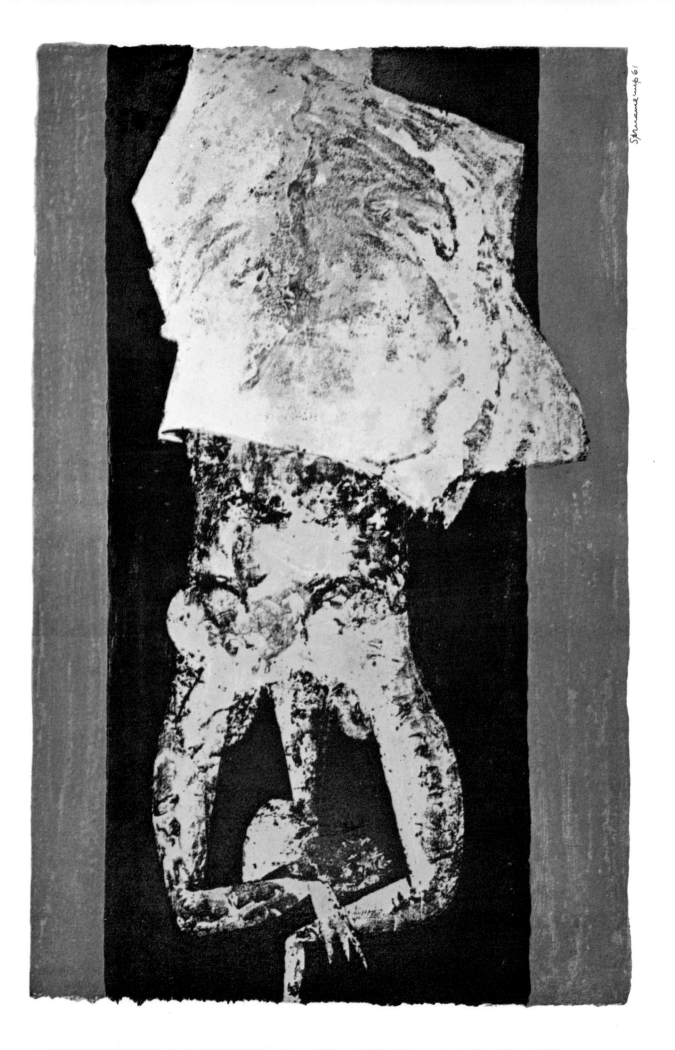

CONSTANTIN (KOSTIA) TERECHKOVITCH

Constantin Terechkovitch was born May 1, 1902, in the environs of Moscow, Russia. His family and acquaintances moved in a cultural circle, and as a young boy he was exposed to the art of the museums of the ancient times, as well as to contemporary movements. At eleven years of age Terechkovitch studied drawing at an academy and at the age of fifteen was admitted, third out of 500, to the school of Beaux Arts of Moscow. Because of the revolution, Terechkovitch left his family and Moscow, and under the most exacting privations he gradually made his way to Paris where his secret spirit sought out the French Impressionists. In his early years at the Café Rotonde, the discussion place of artists of the time, he found the stimulus of great conversation. It was here that he began a lifelong friendship with the artist, Soutine. It was through his association with Soutine that Terechkovitch found the inner Bonnard, and as an artist was liberated to the joy of color.

Terechkovitch is truly a brilliant colorist. His work in painting and in color lithography sings with a plastic quality of color moving in space. These are happy and joyous places, animals, and people that live in the world that his work gives us. Terechkovitch is one of the most distinguished artists of our time, and his work has been acclaimed and treasured wherever people have the privilege of seeing it.

Constantin Terechkovitch
Untitled
ed. 82/100
19¾″ x 25¾″ (vertical)

PAUL WUNDERLICH

Paul Wunderlich was born March 10, 1927, in Berlin, Germany. He did advanced study from 1947 until 1952 at the University for Instructive Art in Hamburg, where he was appointed to the faculty, serving from 1954 until 1960. After extensive travel, Wunderlich lived and maintained a studio in Paris until the end of the year 1961, when he returned to Germany where he now resides. He has won several prizes and awards including the Kunstpreis der Jugend für Graphik in 1960 and the M.S. Collins prize of Philadelphia.

The work of Paul Wunderlich is well known in Europe and the United States. He has had seven one-man exhibitions in the past three years, two of which have been in the United States—one in Philadelphia and one in San Francisco. He has also participated in numerous group exhibitions, and he has illustrated several books, including *Leda* in 1962. Professor Max Bense, in writing of Wunderlich, has said that although Wunderlich has never studied medicine, his work suggests X rays of the human body and distortions of anatomy without giving the concept that the symbols have to do with illness. Wunderlich is a lithographer and painter of great mastery of fantasy and a searching inner vision.

Paul Wunderlich
"Strip Tease"
13/20 edition
25¾" x 19¾" (horizontal)

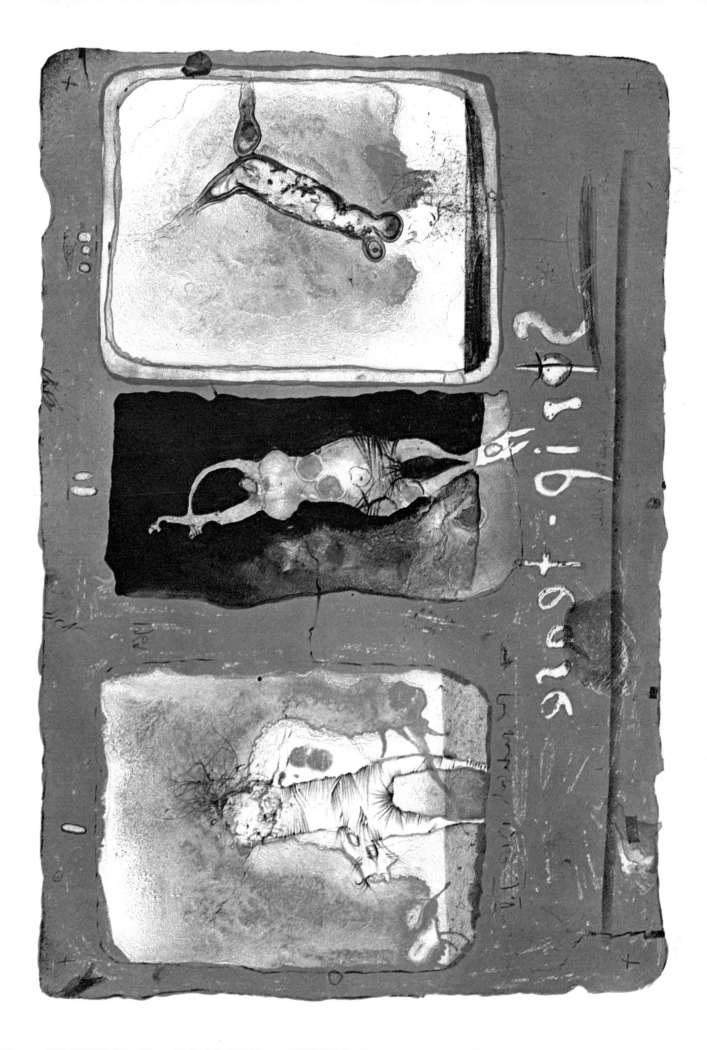

ZAO WOU-KI

Zao Wou-Ki was born in Peking, China, on the 13th of February, 1921. At the age of fifteen, he entered the National School of Hang-Teheou. In 1941 he was appointed a professor of drawing in the same college. During this time Wadime Elisseeff, the curator of the Cernuschi Museum, encouraged Zao Wou-Ki to show his work in Paris. A number of paintings were sent, and Zao Wou-Ki followed them in 1948. The writer and Zao Wou-Ki met for the first time in January of 1949 at an exhibition of collages by Henri Matisse. Subsequently the rapid rise and distinguished career of Zao Wou-Ki have been closely observed.

In his work, painting and lithography have equally shared his attention, and over the past years each follows the same silver thread. The aesthetics of Zao Wou-Ki belong to the realm of magic symbolism, and his work vibrates with strange and beautiful imagery. Substance, such as ships, birds, people, sky, and water, floats in and out of his compositions, which are conceived in endless and continuous space. The legendary concept of the relationship of nature and temporal man plays a basic and significant role. Exhibitions of his work have been held in the most important galleries of the world, and he enjoys an international audience.

Zao Wou-Ki
Proof of the artist
11¼″ x 15″ (vertical)

5

THE STUDIO

IN any discussion of a studio there are two points of view that should be immediately recognized. A "studio" may be any type of place used as a studio, or it may be a place functionally constructed solely for use as a studio. Although I will be speaking about the functionally-constructed studio almost exclusively throughout this chapter, it should be clearly understood at the outset that a large amount of my work has been done in studios of many sorts. A studio is wherever one works, sometimes with the barest facilities. Many times there is a need for improvisation, using items that are not convenient or even adequate. Work has been successfully carried on in basements, barns, lofts, and alleys. Wherever one has the incentive to work and even the barest of equipment, the work can be done. Furthermore, the point in mentioning this is that the work *should* be done. There is nothing gained in waiting around half a lifetime for everything to be "just so." My experience with students and young artists shows that too much time is spent talking about what is needed and what should be done, instead of coming to grips with what is being done.

On two occasions I have helped in establishing workshops for group participation. In both instances, and in others that I have observed, it obviously was not the workshop that produced the work; it was the individuals. Some persons wanted a workshop, and that became the end product. Some were organizers and immediately arranged meetings. Some were dedicated artists, and, with or without the workshop studio, they produced work. It is fine to have a good, well-equipped studio, but it is not the prime factor in producing quality work. In fact, some of the poorest work is produced under the best circumstances. Keep in mind then that we are discussing two situations and that the important objective in each is the aesthetic quality of the work.

Our attention is centered in this chapter on describing the type of studio that each of us has in mind as an environment for working. The studio in which I work is, in my opinion, one of the best of its kind (see Fig. 4). It is adequate in size, so that one feels not only a physical but also an emotional flow of space. The press is the most important piece of equipment and is the nucleus around which the studio is designed. Equipment is arranged in relation to it. The grinding and washing sink is four feet by five feet, press high, constructed out of

Figure 4. Studio as seen from west and south elevation.

wood. It is anchored to the floor, and the interior is covered with fiberglass. It has an adjustable roller bed, so that work may be moved with ease. Under more elaborate conditions, where numerous people are working, a free-standing floor sink would have some advantages. I have worked on both types, and the advantages of the free-standing sink are overshadowed for individual use by the large added cost of construction. Also, it has been found that it is more efficient if one person works at the sink at a time. It is true that a person can work around a free-standing sink and consequently around the work. However, this may also be discounted because of the disadvantage of working at times with the artwork in reverse from bottom to top.

Figure 5.   Relationship of sink to press area.

Heat in the studio should be moderate and controlled. In connection with heat and light it is worth mentioning that, in order to keep the heating cost to a minimum, the daylight source is almost due south in the studio described. There was a choice between a north exposure, which would have given a more even and cooler light, and the southern exposure which was selected. In either case the building could have remained almost the same in design. With the southern exposure the solar radiation has already resulted in a great saving in fuel. It is carefully estimated that this saving in fuel will go a long way toward paying for the building over a 20-year period. During the summer months a flexible butterfly-type awning of plastic material is planned to hold back and redirect the heat rays without altering the light in the studio. The right amount, quality, and direction of light in a critical working space is always at a premium. In this respect the studio should be planned so that it takes the greatest advantage of the existing site. The location and size of the windows, skylights, and free-story windows, or a combination of these, should be planned in relation to the position of equipment in the studio, so that they allow a flood of light to all of the working space.

It is extremely desirable to design the studio on a modular basis in relation to the equipment. The various working heights should be such that the shoulders and back have the least amount of tension and strain. Equipment should be arranged so that there is a flow of direction in the progress of the work from one area to another. It will be noted in Figures 5 and 6 that the various activity centers flow from one place to another without either being cramped or causing bottlenecks in other work areas.

Experience indicates that it is more functional to have a small single ink table of approximately 20 by 28 inches in size. The dimension is slightly larger than the largest roller that is used, and the top can be easily cleaned and quickly changed for different colors. Occasionally it is desirable to have two ink tables in use almost simultaneously. In such instances it is better to have two small ink tables or one that is temporarily improvised on the edge of another counter, rather than one all-purpose large table.

In any studio there should be a great abundance of storage space. One wall of the studio should be devoted to enclosed cupboard space to house the many and various inks and supplies, along with the numerous special items that are acquired along the way. There should also be a place for paper storage which is dust-free and of ample size to hold the several types of paper used in lithography. A rack for pressboards can be built in the close vicinity, since the pressboards are approximately the same size. In the studio described, the storage of stones has beeen very ingeniously worked out, as can be seen in the accompanying photographs (Figs. 7 and 8). Special attention should be directed to the construction, because the design that has been developed sets a new standard for the storage of stones. The rack consists of sections of steel rollers that fit over galvanized pipes, forward and back, which can be adjusted to fit any width stone.

Figure 6.   Flow of space to press area.

Figure 7.　Library stack of stones.

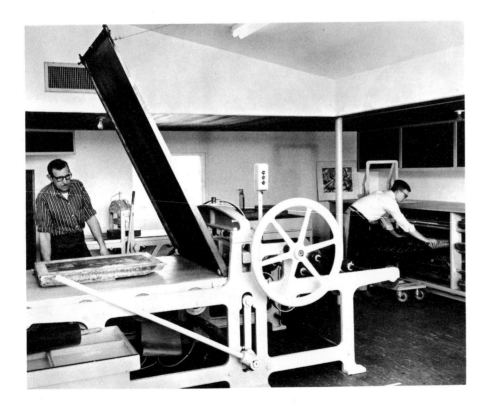

Figure 8.　John Groschner, on left, restacks completed work.

There is, included in the studio, a hydraulic hoist which is completely mobile for transporting stones from one work area to another. This is an extremely important and necessary piece of equipment. After a few years there comes a time when even the smallest stone seems heavy. Some of the stones that I work with are among the largest that have been quarried and weigh 500 pounds or more each. The large press is something of a problem for one person to operate, simply because of its physical size (Fig.9). Because of the amount of force needed, the bed is moved by a motor. However, all other aspects remain the same as the smaller press. Medium to large stones obviously require handling with the major assist of a mechanical hydraulic lift of some type. This equipment takes care of all moving problems without any difficulty whatsoever, and one person can handle the hoist with ease.

The construction of the studio presented some interesting problems. Two factors were outstanding. First, it had to be built within a very limited budget. Second, the relation of major equipment and the need to have it cross-lighted with natural light had to determine to a major degree the interior and exterior appearance. Although nothing is inexpensive, the total cost was held to a minimum by not considering any expensive materials or type of construction. Each decision was determined on the basis of solid construction of a type that could be produced through the use of hand tools. The studio described and illustrated was designed by E. C. Pardon, retired engineer, with the author as collaborator.

6

EQUIPMENT AND MATERIALS

LITHOGRAPHY is planographic as compared to other print mediums. The word "planographic" means that the surface from which the impression is taken is neither raised nor lowered, but that it is pulled from a flat plane. It should be noted again that lithography is based on the simple principle that grease and water will not mix. This premise is actually the basis of lithography. The very simplicity of the medium indicates that there is an area, which is the main body of this book, that requires critical and informed judgments. One is called upon to make these judgments constantly, throughout the working of the medium. Like most simple relationships the complexities that can arise are numerous; each must be recognized, evaluated, and a course determined before serious problems develop.

Lithography is generally worked on limestone. Metal plate, in the form of zinc or aluminum, can be substituted within severe limitations. The stone is uniform in thickness, about three to four inches thick, depending on the size. There are limestone quarries almost everywhere in the world. It is interesting to note in passing, and no small coincidence, that the limestone from the central European area where Senefelder discovered and invented the process has continued throughout the history of lithography to be the best quality stone for use in the medium. In an attempt to reduce the cost of shipping, most limestone quarries have been tested for use. For a number of reasons, such as the density of the stone, the consistency of the texture, and the ability to avoid breaking and fracturing, the stones from central Europe remained the best and as a result were shipped throughout the world.

Stones generally fall into three classifications or grades. They vary in color, and although the color itself has little to do with the properties of the stone, it indicates what the properties are. The most common stone is yellow. It is the softest

Figure 9. Layout of the press for pulling the edition of Knights.

and will not stand up in use very long by comparison to the stones that are more gray in color. Because of the softness, the tooth of the grained surface wears rapidly during work, and consequently, this grade of stone is not used for either fine detail or work which calls for large editions. The middle category or neutral stone is the classification most widely used. This range, which includes many degrees of neutral grayness, is relatively more dense and will hold a tooth for a longer period of time. The last part of a large edition of work pulled from a stone of this classification will be sharper and less fuzzy in appearance than if softer stone is used. This is not too important since most artists pull editions of approximately 50, and it is only when editions of one hundred or more are pulled that the work may lose sharpness. The blue stones, or third classification, include a variety from light blue-gray to what approaches the darkness and hardness of slate.

There is room for a wide variation of opinion as to preference for the type of stone to be worked on. Each stone has its own special characteristics, and although these characteristics can be discussed, they cannot be actually understood until the stones have been used. Then a selection can be made.

Figure 10. Position of hands for grinding using stone method.

I enjoy the overall reaction of the medium neutral gray stone. The reason for this is that my work calls for a rather complex inner relation of various techniques to which the gray stone lends itself best. It will stand reworking and maintain a sharp surface, and at the same time it is not so hard a surface as to limit scraping and gravure. The surface of any type of lithographic stone may be grained so that it is extremely coarse, comparable to the tooth of a rough watercolor paper, or it may be ground in various degrees of fineness, depending on the type of work that is being done (Fig. 10). The stone after grinding is very sensitive to all forms of grease, and it is likewise very absorbent to water.

The prepared stone takes water evenly, if such is the application. The control of these factors becomes critically important.

Any prepared type of grease can be used for drawing or painting on the stone, but for our purposes grease is meant to refer to some form of grease that has a consistently high control factor. In this instance, the grease is in the form of Castile soap, which is very pure, with a predictable and stable reaction. Many experiments have been done with other forms of grease and have proven relatively successful. For example, grease such as axle grease, butter, lard, oil,

Figure 11.   Some tools and materials.

most forms of commercial soap, and numerous other materials have been tested, and they have worked within limitations. The consistency of control is not critical enough, however, to make their use desirable over an extended period. This does not mean that someone may not formulate a new and better formula for drawing and painting in lithography. It merely means that so far the most stabilized formula is the one that is at present produced.

Work is put on the stone with two controlled forms of grease, namely, the formula-prepared lithographic crayon and lithographic tusche. It may seem redundant to restate the word lithographic in referring to numerous materials used; however, it seems necessary because of the accelerated interest in all print mediums. Materials are now manufactured which have the same names and which appear in the same form, but which are not made with the same balanced formula. The lithographic crayon is a solid material in stick or pencil form. Lithographic crayons in America are numbered from 00 through 5. Number 5 is called copal and is extremely hard; softness increases in degrees to 00. In Europe, the numbering is reversed and the lower numbers indicate the harder crayons. Many times an artist will cast his own crayons and make different size sticks for drawing, according to his preference.

Figure 12. *Important components of press.*

Another solid type of material that is used for drawing on stone is rubbing tusche. This is a larger stick than crayon, about one inch square and four inches long. It has more beeswax in it and very little carnauba wax, with a small addition of grease and a slight amount of animal fat. It is very soft and is used, as its name implies, primarily for rubbing on the stone with the fingers or a cloth.

The final and perhaps most important manufactured material for drawing or painting is tusche. It can be used in a drawing manner, but its primary purpose is for painting. It comes in two forms. One a premixed liquid, the other a solid which is mixed with water, turpentine, or gasoline, as is desired, into a substance either thin or thick, depending on the needs and the type of brush to be used with it. The important thing to keep in mind is that with the limited group of described materials any conceivable manner, style, method, or type of application can be produced (Fig. 11).

The next item to be considered is the press. By contrast to the etching press, which has a double roller that creates a continuous type of on and off suction pressure, the lithographic press has a flat horizontal scraper with sliding pressure from the top. The single roller below the bed merely carries the bed of the press. The scraper is fastened in the head of the press, and when pressure is established and the stone is dragged or pulled under the scraper by turning the crank, the print or impression is pulled. This is where the phrase "to pull a print" stems from. Figure 12 shows details of the various working parts. The type of press illustrated is becoming very scarce, and modern substitutes are being manufactured to satisfy the present demand. One cannot be a purist and insist on an old press since they are becoming extinct, but one can insist that the function and quality of performance equal or excel the original form. Until these qualities are established, it would be well to have the contemporary press demonstrated in depth before a purchase is made.

In this connection, at The University of Michigan we had been on the alert for some time for the purchase of an additional old hand lithographic press. When one was located, we lost out on the purchase because of the speed with which it was snapped up by someone who did not need to go through the purchase order procedure. This discouraging experience after several years of search convinced me that if we were to have presses for artists and students it was necessary to design one. Although there are a few modern possibilities, there is only one that is considered the equivalent in performance to an old press, and it does not take advantage of modern technology. Consequently I designed a press that brings this vital equipment up to date. It is economical in cost and

Figure 13. Ink table and related materials.

completely automatic in operation so that women can operate it without the difficulty that they experienced with the old presses.

Although it is not necessary to be a chemist or to have any wide knowledge of chemistry for work in lithography, it might be well to look over a simple chemistry book or to recall some high school chemistry. The materials and process of lithography are based on chemical reactions. A few of the most basic are indicated here so that an attitude may be formed regarding their use. In general, most common inorganic compounds come under the name of acids, bases, salts, and oxides, and these materials are quite widely used in lithography. Although on rare occasions other acids will be referred to, the acids in most regular use are nitric acid and acetic acid. Acids which break apart and ionize almost completely in a water solution are called strong or active acids; of these, nitric acid, HNO_3, is used in the medium. Most acids do not completely ionize in water; such acids are called weak or inactive acids. Acetic acid, as will be noted later, is used for counteretching and is an excellent example of a weak acid.

Gum arabic is included with these materials because of its constant relation to them and because of the chemical reaction that takes place when it combines with limestone, as well as other materials used in the process of lithography. It comes from the acacia tree, which grows in the northwestern part of Africa, and for this reason it is sometimes called gum acacia.

The next major consideration is ink. All inks have a visual similarity; the essential difference in an ink or pigment is the binder. Binders are the materials that are used to hold the molecules of pigment in suspension, so that the mixture is ready for use. In lithography the binders are various slow-drying oils. In hand lithography it is not desirable to have a dryer mixed in the ink as part of the binder. It is better to add the dryer as it is needed at the time of use. The characteristic that one needs to keep in mind at the beginning is that ink, regardless of color, has body. This body is determined by thickness or thinness. Some inks are very soupy or thin. Generally, an ink that has a thick, dense body is preferable (Fig. 13).

Another basic material that needs attention is paper. There are numerous fine papers that may be obtained. A large amount of personal choice enters into the decision on which to use. Papermaking had its infancy in the Orient, and one can still find several examples in that area. Most countries have produced at least one outstanding paper. Other than personal preference, there are basic characteristics that should be observed. A paper for the lithography of artists must have body, thickness, softness, pureness, and longevity. These characteristics require that it be made of rag, under the most exacting and rigid control, by paper houses whose pride in their watermark would not allow an inferior product to be released. Perhaps it is a mistake to mention specific names because there are so many. It would be a greater mistake not to let the reader know what preference has been established from experience. The following list is not stated in the order of preference: Shogun, Natsume, Kochi, Inomachi, Cobham, Roma, Fabiano Book, Umbria, Crown and Sceptre, Arnold, Arches, and Rives B.K.F. I am intimately acquainted with each of these papers; however, there are other fine papers. There are times when one is more suitable to a particular work than another. By using the highest quality paper one may be sure that the work will remain unchanged for generations.

It is hoped that the reader will allow this to suffice as a brief introduction to the basic studio materials and equipment, and that we may proceed with this as a frame of reference to examine each item in detail throughout the remainder of our discussion of equipment and materials used in the making of a lithograph.

Emil Weddige
Wall Section, 9 Quai de Bourbon
edition 40   B.K.F. Rives paper
25¾" x 19¾" (horizontal)

24/40   Wallcollection Quer de Bourbon   Emil Waldige

7

SOME CHEMICAL REACTIONS

THE limestone used in lithography in its natural state at the time it is quarried is equally sensitive to both grease and water. In other words, it accepts both separately with complete affinity. Technically one would say that in its original state limestone has the dual properties of being hydrophilic and lipophilic. These words are derived from the Greek: "-philic" from the Greek *philos*, meaning liking or affection, "hydro-" referring to water, and "lipo-" referring to grease. The crayon and the tusche, as mentioned earlier, are composed of a formula of carnauba wax, a very hard and dense wax; purified beeswax, a soft wax; lampblack; and Castile soap. The lampblack, a completely inert substance, has no other function to perform than to visually show the precise amount of Castile soap that is deposited during painting or drawing. The Castile soap is considered in this instance as a form of pure grease, or so nearly so that one-tenth of one percent is overlooked. The balance between the amount of beeswax and carnauba wax determines the degree of hardness or softness in the crayon. From this proportion the number of the crayon is arrived at; for example, an American crayon No. 4 has the same ingredients as a No. 3 crayon except for the proportions. The No. 3 has one-half of one part more Castile soap; whereas the No. 4 has more carnauba wax and proportionately less Castile soap, and consequently it is harder. It is very important to keep in mind that this balance is critical and must be understood in order that it can be maintained throughout the entire process of lithography. An examination of the tests starting on page 124 will show more clearly the balanced relationships of these materials.

Currently there is an epidemic of recommending lithographic crayons and lithographic tusche for numerous other purposes such as batik and silk screen. This is sheer nonsense because mediums other than lithography do not require a precisely-balanced formula of ingredients. A much less expensive and more direct formula could be used in all instances except when used in lithography. I have no particular quarrel with materials being used in any way that anyone chooses to use them; however, I do condemn the present practice of new manufacturers, on a Johnny-come-lately basis, of entering the scene with both crayons and tusche that are not labeled properly for the uninitiated. Either these materials should be formulated to exact standards, or they should have distinguishing labels. Keep in mind that the ingredients themselves are very inexpensive. What one is really purchasing is the extreme care and exact control that is exercised over the formula, which is of the utmost importance to the lithographer. In fact, within this overall relationship of balances, the sensitization of the stones, the formula of crayon and tusche, the grease content of the pigment, and the ability to maintain an even water relationship throughout until the edition is completed is where the novice is separated from the serious student or professional working in the medium. With this introduction we can now go back and complete the observations on the part that chemistry plays in the combined relationships.

When the stone has been sensitized through the grinding preparation, it is equally in a hydrophilic and lipophilic condition. The painting and drawing is done on the stone with crayon and tusche, which, as mentioned, is a balanced formula containing grease. After the artwork is completed, it receives the first preparation which consists of dusting the stone with French chalk which adheres to the areas of crayon and tusche and helps to make them more resistant to any corrosive action. This is followed by dusting with powdered resin which has the function of helping to form a bond of adhesion between all of the ingredients, including gum arabic applied in the next phase. After the dusting, gum arabic, in a solution of water combined with a small percentage of nitric acid, is wiped or brushed liberally over the entire face of the stone and kept moving for about four minutes. (Chapter 11 further explains the gum arabic and acid solution.) The excess is then cupped off with the side of the hand, leaving a rather full coating on the stone. This application of gum arabic and nitric acid is repeated for approximately the same length of time and cupped off with the hand, leaving a full but not excessive layer.

The stone is then put to rest for approximately 12 hours. The time may be slightly extended without ill effects, providing not too strong an acid solution has been used. It can be shortened in many instances to about one-half that time without damage; however, it must be borne in mind at this phase that anything more or less than 12 hours involves a calculated risk. I have seen this risk taken time and again with a loss, unfortunately, of the finest values that distinguish an excellent print. It is well to keep in mind that it is easy to print dark but it is not easy to hold the stone in the manner in which it was conceived. One could make this as an almost covering observation, so be cautious of falling into the trap of overanxiety.

When the solution of gum arabic and nitric acid is applied to the stone for the first time, there are several things that happen instantaneously. The gum arabic separates the grease from the carnauba wax, beeswax, and lampblack and impregnates the grease into the stone in exactly the same manner and to precisely the same degree that it was put on during the painting or drawing stage. Next, the small amount of nitric acid performs two functions. It acts as a helping agent to the gum arabic by liberating a small amount of carbon-dioxide gas, and its corrosive action cleans the stone of any small amount of smudge or dirt that has accidentally accumulated during the painting phase. The chemical reaction of the combination of all the ingredients with the calcium content of the limestone makes the unworked or open areas of the stone lipophobic, while the areas containing positive grease are made hydrophobic. Finally a small amount of the calcium, magnesium, potassium salts, and the gum arabic combine with the resin to form, in combination with the liberated calcium, an even impregnation of solidified substances. This, in effect, makes the unworked areas of the stone slightly darker and harder than before they were treated.

It will be observed after a little experience that when employing mixed techniques it is much easier to work with a knife, a graver, or razor blade on the stone before any preparation of the stone has taken place. It is further observed in connection with the preparation of the stone that a student frequently assumes that, since the preparation is critically important, greater success can be ensured by either continuing the process longer or by using larger amounts of the materials. Both of these assumptions are incorrect. The action as stated is instantaneous, and what is going to happen from the materials is immediate. Simply proceeding longer or with more materials will not alter what has been established at first contact.

Adding a stronger solution of acid to the gum is also a usual error. Certainly it will appear more active on the stone; however, the activity is the most certain destruction of the fine characteristics of the work. In fact, pure nitric acid, given time, would completely destroy the stone. Under the chapter on Methods and Special Techniques, a few variations will be analyzed for unique or extraordinary situations.

The observations discussed in this chapter are of basic and critical importance to the lithographer. It is essential that one understand what should happen in order to determine and evaluate the condition of the stone and the work throughout the entire operation. These details should be constantly referred to in conjunction with the studio work until the reaction and timing become second nature. Since none of the reactions are obvious during this phase of the process, many will have to be taken on faith until one is acquainted with the very subtle indications from which to form judgments. In a small edition it is possible to obtain fair results with a medium quality preparation. Even in the hands of an expert a stone with a medium quality preparation will require careful juggling throughout to have a uniform appearance for an edition of even average size. In a large edition it is not possible to obtain fair printing results with a poorly prepared stone. The work will print unevenly, and in spite of the greatest care in cleaning and doctoring, it will gradually become brutal and coarse. On the other hand, when a stone is prepared properly, it is almost impossible to experience anything except beautiful, even printing.

Emil Weddige
"Table With Apples"
edition 30
25¾" x 19¾" (horizontal)

9/30   Table with apples   Enid Wardois

8

INKS AND RELATED MATERIALS

GOOD ink, made especially for hand lithography, is ground with very slow-drying oil and no driers, and it has a thick or dense body. The ink, when it is received, is just about as lean and neutral in comparison to the grease content of the crayon or tusche as is possible. Also, it is generally as tacky as is normally possible and is as flat as the pigment itself will allow. Tackiness is a critically important characteristic of ink because the ink must have a type of tackiness or ability to stick and to transfer its body from one surface to another. Body also implies thixotropy or the ability to alter or change the apparent composition but hold a basic density upon being worked or reworked. The ink warms up with friction and becomes soft and pliable. Some inks react too much in this manner and after one-half to three-quarters of an hour of working become so soft that it is impossible to prevent scum.

Along with these properties, the ink must have a balance of grease content related to the crayon or tusche. The lithographer, as will be noted, has several qualities of the ink pigment which he can control—the body, tackiness, thixotropy, sheen, stiffness, or grease content. Control is exercised by the addition of materials closely related to inks—standard linseed oil, thickened linseed oil, varnish No. 2 or No. 3, standard varnish No. 9 or No. 10, a mordant or sun-thickened varnish No. 10, No. 470 oil, and magnesium carbonate. The artist lithographer should consider these items in the same manner that an artist painter considers the various binders and vehicles that are normally used in relation to oil pigment for painting purposes. If one thinks of them in this manner, it will be quite easy to understand the ink pigment used, and normally referred to as ink, in lithography. Importance is placed upon this understanding because if a lithographer limits himself to using ink pigment only as it comes from the manufacturer with just sufficient vehicle to make it workable for use, then the medium of lithography and the range of its possibilities fall far short of what they should be.

Whenever the opportunity presents itself and discarded ink pigment is available, experiments should be conducted in which the various ingredients named are mixed with the ink in as many ways as possible to find out precisely what happens, rather than wait for the actual time of printing to attempt to arrive at a balanced ink. Keep in mind essentially that the ink must have tackiness in order to be transported from the stone to the paper and that it must also have body in order to hold detail and edges. Along with these characteristics, an ink pigment for hand lithography must have long-lasting qualities in order to conform to the high standards of art. Let us examine some of the ways a lithographer is able to adjust his pigment or ink.

We are familiar with linseed oil, an extremely greasy substance. If the work on the stone is too lean because of either a very hard crayon, very light work, because the etch has been too strong, or for any reason the work on the stone needs to be brought up more, then it is advisable to attempt to increase the grease content of the work on the stone by the addition of linseed oil to the ink pigment. In terms of ink, the linseed oil has no body properties and is a thinning agent.

Varnish No. 3 is a fairly thin varnish and will add the property of gloss to the extent that it is put into the ink. It will add some tackiness but no body. If a very transparent color is desired that is also very light in value, an amount of varnish No. 3 or No. 4 is required along with a transparent base. The addition of No. 10 varnish is recommended if less transparent base is used. The transparent base in itself is as neutral or slightly more neutral than the pigment.

Recalling our knowledge of watercolor in terms of a transparent medium, a tint of watercolor is made by adding a transparent material—water. This separates the molecules of pigment and spreads them over a wider area, and the effect is a lighter value. The same thing is true in lithography except that various oils and varnishes are substituted for water. For example, if we want a lighter black, it is necessary to add whatever amount of transparent base is desired in terms of gray transparency. This is true of all the ink pigments, in terms of color, that are used in lithography. One may by choice consider the medium from entirely a transparent standpoint or conversely from entirely an opaque standpoint, or as many times happens, a combination from transparent to opaque, including translucency. This may seem quite complex at first reading, but I should remind you that this is the attitude that you normally take in either watercolor painting or oil painting.

In a mixture of black or color and transparent base, since the transparent base is a nongrease mixture, it would be normal at this point to add a few drops of linseed oil which would tend to re-establish the balance of greasiness in relation to the grease content of the crayon and tusche. Supposing, for example, that it was desired to have a gloss black, as well as a transparent black. In this instance, a division would have to be determined between an amount of transparent base and an amount of varnish. Varnish No. 3, a softer varnish, is recommended. This would give to the pigment a greater sheen, as well as a greater toughness. If a relatively flat surface is desired instead of a gloss or semigloss surface, it would be necessary to eliminate the linseed oil and in its place use oil No. 470, which is a thin liquid, thinner and less greasy than linseed oil. If the balance of the grease content is disturbed so much with oil No. 470 that the work on the stone does not come up full, a slight amount of linseed oil is needed to re-establish the balance.

There also may be times when a completely mat finish, not only of black but of any color, is desirable. In cases of this type the ink pigment is mixed either with the transparent base or the opaque white, whichever is desirable for the particular problem, and to this bulk is added about one-third magnesium carbonate. When this has been folded in and thoroughly mixed, pull a trial proof in order to determine how much linseed oil will be needed to restore greasiness, so that the work comes up full. When the balance is established, the ink pigment when printed will give a completely mat finish. It is repeated that the procedure is the same for black, as well as for all colors.

Since we will be using the terms vehicle and binder, it would be advisable to define these words so that we are in complete understanding. A binder in oil pigment is ground so that each molecule of pigment is surrounded by a molecule of oil. This is true for paints used in oil painting, as well as for pigments used in lithography.

On the other hand, a vehicle is any substance that can be used as either a diluent or as an extender within the family of oil. Many vehicles are utilized in oil paints and in the ink pigments used in lithography. For example, a vehicle in lithography could be gasoline, kerosene, benzine, turpentine, various thicknesses of linseed oils, or various varnishes. Any of these will act as a vehicle diluent or extender to establish particular characteristics. To summarize, we must keep in mind that the balance of these vehicles with the pigment will be related to the grease content that has been deposited through the work on the stone.

When any ink is broken down on the ink slab with the spatula and worked thoroughly, it will bring the ink to nearly the same consistency that it was at the time of manufacture. It will be noticed that it becomes slightly softer than before the working. The friction or warming up of the ink through manipulation brings it to this state. This is normal and to be expected. However, if the friction of work through ink-rolling and so on, continues to soften the ink and it becomes rather soupy, it may be concluded that it was not manufactured for hand-press work. An ink with too great a thinning behavior pattern should be considered a poor ink for hand lithography, and it is recommended that it be discarded rather than attempt to re-establish a balance. Under forced conditions a balance of this type of ink has been attempted, and it must be confessed that it was not a very pleasant experience.

There are occasions when one finds that a color ink has within its natural characteristics of pigment a tendency to become softer and soluble in water, leaving a film both on the work and on the water. This is a slightly different situation because within a manufactured ink, such as any of a number of quality inks, one may find a red or a violet or occasionally a green or a yellow pigment that shows these characteristics. Within this category, applying particularly to the reds, there are one or two magnificent reds that are not obtainable in any other form but which in themselves are slightly water soluble and have a strong tendency to become too thin. There is nothing much that can be done about this problem if they are used except to bring into play the mordant or sun-thickened No. 10 varnish which has been referred to. To establish some idea here as to amount, let us assume that we have on the slab about two tablespoons of red ink that is scumming when rolled on the stone and also showing up red on the sponge or on the printed paper. Unless this undesirable characteristic is eliminated, it is impossible to do a creditable job of printing. To the two tablespoons of ink, add about the size of a small lima bean of either sun-thickened No. 10 varnish or, preferably, the mordant varnish. This material has about the tackiness of flypaper; you will find that once it is on the ink spatula, it is difficult to get off into the ink. In other words, it is emphasized that this material is so tacky that it takes a great deal of mixing in order to blend it into the body of the ink. Once it has been thoroughly mixed, it brings the tackiness of the ink back sufficiently so that there is a possibility of maintaining printing quality.

As we proceed and later discuss color printing, what has been said here in terms of ink will be slightly enlarged, but I would like to make it very clear that there is no formula for mixing an ink. The one thing we know as a guide is that there is the desired balance between the grease content of the ink and the work on the stone, and this is easily seen from the proof. If the ink is not in balance, the work will be too light, too dark, or it will scum or fill; and adjustments must be tested. With the ingredients that have been discussed, the problem is to experiment and find the balance that is most suitable to the particular job on hand. Keep in mind that every lithograph will call for a slightly different balance of these ingredients and yet arrives at the same proportion of grease content. The proof is always the quality and consistency of the printing.

Emil Weddige
"Mountain Meadow"
edition 12
30" x 22½" (horizontal)

9

PREPARING THE STONE

THE lithographic stone is selected according to the size of the artwork that is contemplated. There should be approximately one and one-half inches on the margins of the work. This allows the scraper to fit within the dimension of the stone and at the same time be larger than the artwork. The size of the scraper should be slightly larger than the dimension of the work and generally is stated as being off the work and on the stone. It should not be over the edge of the stone or larger than the printing dimension of the stone. When the scraper is larger than the printing dimension of the stone and hangs over the edge, the scraper is damaged at the point of the overhang. The damage will appear both in the leather and the wood of the scraper. This damage is easily understood when one considers that when printing takes place, there is more than a 1000 pounds of pressure per square inch where the scraper is on the stone, and if the scraper hangs over the stone, there is a reverse diagonal from that point to zero pounds. Hence, at the edge or at the diminishing apex point of overhang, there will be a mark or line pressed both into the leather and into the wood of the scraper where the change takes place between the pressure force and the nonpressure force. Consequently, the scraper is damaged.

Should this damaged scraper later be used on a larger piece of artwork, a line or blurred printing mark would show in the new work where none was desired. If for some personal reason the full stone is printed, the scraper should be taken apart and repaired after each edition is pulled. One other note regarding the scraper. A very small scraper should never be used on a large stone regardless of the size of the artwork. This will break the stone without fail.

The next consideration is the type or quality of stone most desirable for the artwork. This depends to some degree on experience; however, a rule of thumb would be that if there is very fine work and a great deal of detail in the contemplated art, a harder stone would be preferable. If, conversely, the artwork includes a quantity of crayon, the softer stone may be more desirable.

After the selection of the stone has been made, the stone is placed on the grinding table or wash rack. If there is ink on the stone from previous work, it should be washed off thoroughly with turpentine because the old ink will coagulate

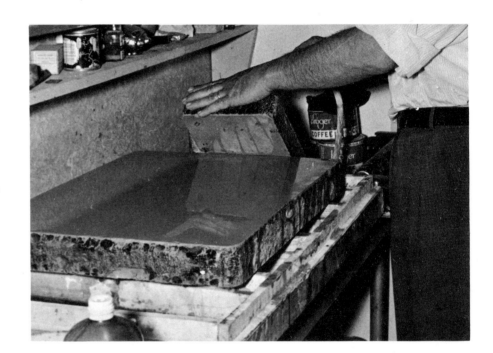

Figure 14.   Beginning of grinding.

during the grinding and mix into the grinding compound and cause excessive and many times uneven grindings. After the turpentine washing has been completed, thoroughly wash all equipment and the stone with water, so that everything is completely clean. Particular attention is specified for washing. The stone is washed thoroughly on the face and on the edges where old gum may have collected. Old gum dissolves slowly and can desensitize a streak in the stone if it should be dragged across the stone by capillary action toward the end of the grinding. This is a good time to file and polish the edges with pumice stone so that they are slightly rounded.

It is recommended that the hands be rinsed continually so that at and during the time of actual grinding all types of foreign grit have been thoroughly removed. Keep in mind that one particle of No. 200 grit, which is almost impossible to see, will, when mixed into a quantity of No. F grit, make the wildest pattern of scratches you have ever seen. The washing procedure cannot be overemphasized because it has been observed time and again in the grinding preparation of a stone that it is extremely easy to be just a slight bit careless and develop scratches in the stone that can only be removed by continued grindings (Figs. 14 and 15).

There are two methods of grinding for the facing of a stone. One is to use a levigator, which is essentially a round disc of cast iron with three or four oscillating holes, plus a handle. This levigator may vary in size and weight; however, it is found that a fifteen-pound levigator is most effective for continuous grinding and produces the least amount of fatigue for the arms during the grinding period. It is heavy enough to perform the function of grinding, and it oscillates well when manipulated by the general strength of the arm of an average person. There is a great deal of latitude, but the same weight levigator works well for a light person of 110 pounds and is equally effective for a heavier person.

Besides the hand type there are also various power-driven levigators. These range from the large fixed parallel grinders, as used in marble factories, to motor-driven flexible shaft disc levigators. A general observation on motor-driven levigators is that the lithographic stones are used up too fast by power grinding in the hands of inexperienced operators, and much more stone is ground off than is usually necessary. This happens for various reasons. The most important of these being that unless a fixed parallel type is used there is a profuse number of scratches that are put into the stone because of the force that is moving the iron disc against the surface of the stone. The result is extended grinding and loss of stone. These scratches are not caused by dirt or foreign matter as are those described earlier. They are caused instead by the sheer force of the iron against the stone at the rapid start of the action of the motor, contrasted to the slow start when the arm operates the levigator and gradually builds up normal grinding speed. If the flexible shaft power grinder is controlled by a set or automatic rheostat, then this tool comes close to the quality of hand grinding and is an excellent labor-saving device. However, the type of power levigator that is feasible for artists' lithographic studios is expensive and not better than the hand method. The time is coming when stones will be much more scarce and expensive than they are now, and it is recommended, regardless of the method, that a minimum amount of stone be ground off during the surfacing.

The second method of grinding is with two stones face to face, using a smaller stone of approximately the same weight as the levigator. In this method the upper stone is moved in a figure-eight pattern. (Note the pattern in Fig. 16.)

Generally for each method there should be three grindings for the preparation of a stone. Avoid any weight other than the weight of the stone or levigator in performing the grinding. During the grinding the hands should not be in any position where they will exercise more weight or pressure at one point than at any other point; if they do, the stone will be ground unevenly; and the correction of an unevenly ground stone is a long process. You will notice after

Figure 16. Pattern of grinding.

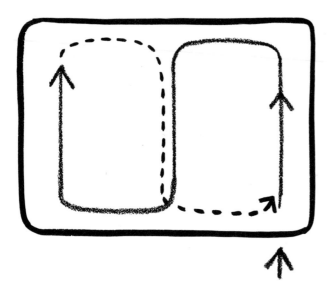

Figure 17. Pattern of surfacing.

the first grinding that the old work is ground off more in some areas than in others. This is a normal happening and should be disregarded. Follow the pattern of grinding, each time covering the entire face of the stone throughout each grinding period. It will also be noticed, with either the levigator or the facing-stone method, that when either goes over the edge of the stone being ground, near or past the center, that there is a different sound. This harsher grinding sound is caused because the balance of weight has begun to be outward rather than flat. This should and can easily be avoided. The levigator or facing stone, depending on the method, should extend approximately one-third over the edges, whenever the pattern of grinding includes the edges. There is a slight latitude; however, it is wise to establish an approximate one-third pattern for grinding. This will avoid rounding the edges or grinding the stone convexly.

With this information in mind we are now ready to grind or resurface a stone. The stone is placed on the bed of the grinding rack at a convenient distance back and parallel to the front. Extend the arms out over the stone only within easy reaching distance, so that there is no cramping from the forward-to-backward movement. This is important because, without knowing, it is easy to exercise more pressure at one point than at another when there is an uneven reach. Generally, the first grinding is made with a coarser compound, and the remaining two grindings are with a finer compound. The latter will produce the type of grain surface that has been predetermined. On rare occasions it is necessary, because of deep scratches in the previous work, to extend this surfacing operation to four grindings. In such instances divide the number of coarser and finer grindings. The grinding time varies a great deal with the kind of moisture in the air and the temperature; however, it generally takes approximately 10 to 15 minutes for each of the three grindings for a medium-sized stone.

The stone should be dampened thoroughly with water. The excess water is then cupped off with the hand, leaving the stone fairly well flooded but not overflowing. On this dampened surface sprinkle about one-half teaspoonful of grinding compound, then place either the levigator or grinding stone flatly on top, and the oscillating pattern is begun (Fig. 17). If there is too much water on the stone, the grinding compound will overflow into the sink and will be wasted. If there is too little water, there is no lubricant to carry the grinding compound, and the faces of the two surfaces will begin to stick before the actual grinding has been completed. Experiment with the amount of water, and adjust to the requirements. As the grinding continues, there will come a time when everything will seem very slippery and soapy. Nothing

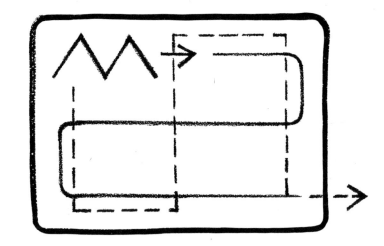

Figure 18. Pattern for putting on sharp tooth.

much is happening at this point, and you are apt to think that the material is not functioning. However, ignore this reaction and continue to grind, and you will soon get out of this particular cycle and into one where you can again hear the compound biting into the stone. This is the cycle when the most effective grinding is actually taking place. As you proceed there will be formed a fairly heavy sludge of white powder. Continue grinding until the two surfaces—the stone that is being ground and the grinder that is being used—become sticky and slower to move. When this begins to happen, remove the levigator or facing stone by working it gradually to the side and thence off the stone that is being ground. Wash everything thoroughly. If one should go on grinding or leave the work at the point where it becomes sticky, the two flat surfaces would become cemented together.

After everything is washed carefully, proceed to the second grinding. When the second grinding is finished, and everything has been washed, the stone should be carefully examined to see that it is without scratches. At this time also take a steel straight edge and place it corner to corner to determine that the stone is flat, neither concave nor convex. If everything seems satisfactory, proceed with the final grinding. When this is completed to the point where you sense from your previous experience that it is about to become sticky, then put on a final sharp tooth. In the case of the levigator one merely moves more slowly with the same pattern. In the case of the stone-against-stone grinding, a shorter zig-zag motion is performed instead of the larger oscillation pattern

Figure 19.   Final washing at an angle to prevent capillary action from edges.

(see Fig. 18). This phase should be continued for about three to five minutes. When finished, the stone or levigator is removed by working it off the edge, and everything is flushed and washed thoroughly with water. The stone should now be propped up at an angle with a piece of wood under one edge so that it will drain. When it is in the position of draining, it should again be flushed gently, keeping the stream of water slightly away from the upper edge so that capillary action will not pull any excess dirt from the top or sides of the stone (see Fig. 19). The stone should now be allowed to dry. If one is in a hurry, the water can be removed with a rubber window squeegee; and the stone fanned dry, but this is not necessary. When the stone is dry, it is ready for work.

If work is going to proceed immediately, the stone is transported to the drawing area. If it is going to be used later, a clean piece of paper, such as an unused newsprint paper, should be placed over the face of the stone and fastened down with Scotch tape. The stone in this prepared form has become sensitized equally to grease and water, consistently throughout its entire surface. It is in the purest form that the stone can be in, and any careless handling carries with it a penalty. There is a tendency to feel tense and protective before the first brush or crayon mark is made on this fresh stone. This need not be the case, simply keep in mind that the purpose of grinding the stone is not only to clean it but to sensitize it both to water and grease and that any moisture or grease will detract from the state that you have been very careful to produce. The stone is now ready to receive the painting.

10

CRAYON AND TUSCHE

These examples were drawn with Wm. Korn crayons—copal and Nos. 4 through 0. The stone had a very fine grain of 3F, produced with graining quartz. In each example the pressure against the stone with all crayons was approximately the same. Starting from the top and reading in order, the group of fine lines on the right of each example were produced by a two-directional movement, gradually becoming stronger until the visual strength of the crayon was about the same on each test. The area on the left was made with the flat side of the various crayons, maintaining the same pressure for each example. The area in the center was made with increasing pressure until the crayon was forced to break. Your attention is called to the numbering of the crayons. European crayons are marked in reverse of those manufactured in America.

A few observations are interesting. The size of the grain of the stone had a definite relationship to the classification of the crayon. The harder crayons worked better on fine grain, and conversely, the soft crayons, especially Nos. 1 and 0, were too soft and had a tendency to slide or slip. Also in this connection, the softer crayons had a tendency to fill and take unevenly. The finest lines had a tendency to break and could not withstand a standard preparation in an even manner. Copal showed the weakest characteristics when used for very light lines.

EXAMPLE 1

EXAMPLE 4

EXAMPLE 2

EXAMPLE 5

EXAMPLE 3

EXAMPLE 6

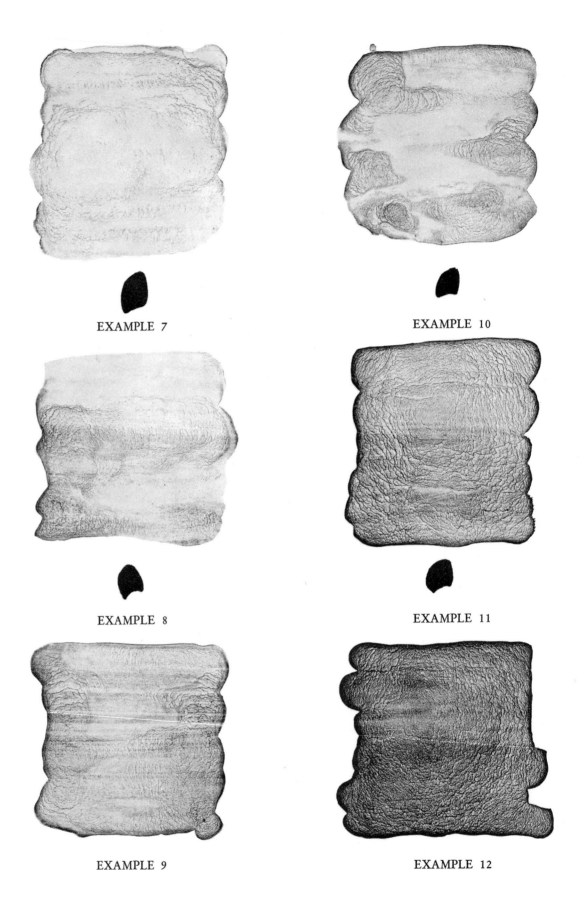

EXAMPLE 7

EXAMPLE 10

EXAMPLE 8

EXAMPLE 11

EXAMPLE 9

EXAMPLE 12

EXAMPLES 7–12

In this series of tests, as well as the preceding ones, the intention was to try to work both lighter and darker than normal to determine where the technique broke down. A stone with the same grain as in the first tests was used, but in this instance it was a harder and slightly more gray type of stone. One hundred and thirty drops of distilled water at room temperature were used. Twenty drops of tusche were added to the water. The tusche, Korns in stick form, was also prepared with distilled water. The consistency of the tusche was dense, so that one spot would produce a solid black when applied separately. This is noted in the spot that was placed in the middle of the tests. It was liquid enough, however, to allow the easy use of a dropper. It was anticipated that Example 7 would be excessively light and wash out in an irregular manner. This proved correct. Five additional drops of tusche were added to the mixture for Example 8 and 5 additional drops for Example 9 or a total of 30 drops of tusche at this point. Example 10 was increased by 5 drops of tusche, and Example 11 was increased by 10 drops or a total of 45 drops. Finally, Example 12 was increased by 15 drops of tusche, making an overall total of 60 drops. Very little of the combined mixture was used in the total group, so it would be fairly safe to say that the original amount of water remained within 15 drops. Another way of stating the equation would be that 130 minus 15 drops of water could have been the starting point if the examination had started with 60 drops of tusche.

It should be noted that there are many ways of applying tusche, and the effect and the mixture will vary greatly, depending on the method used. In this group a very soft camel's-hair brush of one-half-inch diameter was used. The brush in each instance had a medium load of the tusche-water mixture. A very light touch was used in applying the tusche. The brush was glided over the stone, barely touching the surface, and kept in constant motion. At the edges of each area where the brush moved more slowly in making the turn, it is noted that the deposit of tusche is more dense and consequently darker. This type of application will always show the pattern of settling if allowed to dry without disturbance. It is further observed that the mixture as indicated must be applied rapidly; otherwise, the deposit is relatively darker.

EXAMPLES 13–18

The tusche mixture used for these examples consisted of 100 drops of distilled water and started with 20 drops of stick tusche, mixed as previously stated. In Examples 13, 14, and 15, the tusche was applied with a clean cloth to a dry stone, and in Examples 16, 17, and 18 it was applied with the tip of a one-half-inch camel's-hair brush to a pre-water-dampened stone. The work was done

EXAMPLE 13

EXAMPLE 16

EXAMPLE 14

EXAMPLE 17

EXAMPLE 15

EXAMPLE 18

in pairs, light to dark. First, the area on the right was dampened fully with a perfectly clean brush and water. Then, working rapidly to avoid drying change, the area on the left was lightly painted with a clean cloth wrapped around a finger and dipped into the tusche mixture. Because of the absorption of the cloth, a timing sense had to be developed to determine the possible size of area that could be painted. As with a brush, it is necessary to pick up more of the tusche mixture for a larger area. In this case, one application to the cloth was all that was needed.

On completion, a loaded brush was immediately applied to the adjacent water-dampened area; the brush point was put into contact in several places with the water but did not touch the stone. Because of the weight of the mixture and the pull of gravity on the brush, the tusche made a flow outward from each point of application. In Examples 14 and 17 the tusche mixture was increased with 10 drops of tusche. Examples 15 and 18 were made with an additional 20 drops of tusche. The application in each pair of examples was constant. Attention is directed to the three cloth applications where the manner of execution is suggested from the appearance.

EXAMPLES 19–24

Examples 19 to 24 show six gradations of rubbing tusche. These were applied with a small cotton cloth, wrapped around the index finger. They were casually done, without attention to evenness of the individual areas. Rubbing tusche is also numbered as to hardness or softness; however, it is formulated to a softer index in comparison with crayons. The reason for this is obvious since the material is not generally applied directly to the stone. The rubbing tusche used in these examples was No. 3 throughout, and the grain of the stone was coarse No. 180. Application was made in a polydirectional manner, first in a circular movement, then from horizontal to vertical, and then back to a circular movement. On examination it will be noticed that a few streaks stand out, indicating a slightly heavier or fresh charge of tusche. In Examples 20 and 23 a No. 2 crayon by Charbonnel (foreign classification) was drawn on top of the rubbed area. It is noted that, although approximately the same pressure was used, the crayon mark is darker on the darker ground. The reason for this is that there was sufficient rubbing tusche on the darker ground to mix or combine with the crayon and actually make a broader, darker line.

In Examples 21 and 24 a wash of water-liquid tusche was applied with a soft, lightly-loaded brush. Example 21 was done with a mixture of 100 drops of distilled water and 20 drops of prepared tusche. These examples were painted with one brush load, and when dry, the brushed areas were extremely light in contrast to the rubbed area. The largest of the brush areas was painted first, then the medium, and finally the smallest area. It will be noticed that the first or

EXAMPLE 19

EXAMPLE 22

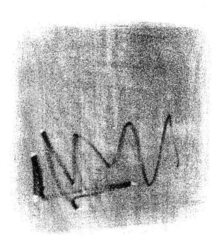

EXAMPLE 20

EXAMPLE 23

EXAMPLE 21

EXAMPLE 24

fresh brush mark is stronger. This indicates how rapidly a change in value takes place. It was anticipated that the liquid tusche brush marks would gain slightly in darkness, and they were made relatively lighter to compensate. Liquid tusche always has a definite tendency to gain. In this instance it was also painted over another grease surface. It is well to keep this observation in mind when using liquid tusche.

It is easy to paint blacks, but careful compensation to a lighter mixture must be made to obtain grays. Example 24 was painted immediately afterwards with the same mixture of liquid tusche as in Example 21. Although the brushed areas are a dark gray and not black, they are very close to black, which again dramatically shows the gain that takes place when painting is done over another area. Although it is known from experience that a very light wash will take on the character of the ground, the proof, as in this example, is always amazing. When an artist or student is working with me and says at the proofing stage, "This is much too dark, that is not the way I painted it," the statement is incorrect. The fact is that it was the way it was painted in terms of the amount of grease deposited.

We must learn to separate visual values in various types of applications and compensate for their characteristics. Otherwise, what generally happens is that an attempt is made on the stone to compensate at the proof state, and any procedure used at this time is definitely a distant second best. The procedure for compensation will be discussed in detail under the chapter on Methods and Special Techniques. For the present it is indicated that unless compensation is made in dealing with mixed techniques, the freshness of the grays will become coarse and will be actually lost. They may appear as gray merely through the principle of producing visual gray through separation of black spots and white paper and not through the actual gray of value. The areas will function to some extent but not in terms of light values.

EXAMPLES 25–30

Tusche can be applied in as many ways as one can imagine. For the purpose here, it was desired to try an experiment in a manner that was unusual and would add an additional unknown. The unknown became to me the most interesting aspect of the examination. Perhaps the best way of describing this unknown is to say that the freshly ground stone was intentionally soiled before the crayon and tusche application. The stone was ground with 1F. The areas for application were determined, and then they were lightly wiped with a water-dampened sponge, using vertical strokes. The sponge used was one that had been in regular use for general dampening. It should be noted that no attempt was made to select a dirty sponge and that the one used was rinsed several times in clean water before being employed in the test. After dampen-

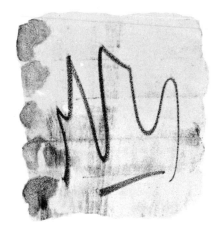

EXAMPLE 25

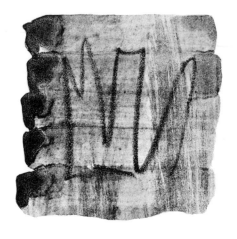

EXAMPLE 28

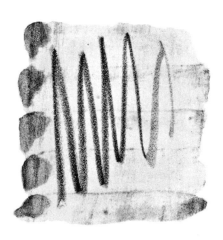

EXAMPLE 26

EXAMPLE 29

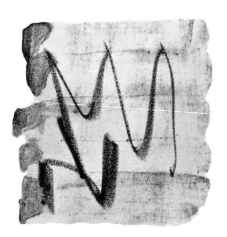

EXAMPLE 27

EXAMPLE 30

ing, the stone was fanned dry, and no difference in the appearance of the stone could be detected. The question to be determined was, "Did the sponge have any traces of gum arabic remaining, even after repeated rinsing?" The crayon used for the line was Korn No. 3 throughout, and the pressure in each instance was approximately the same with slight variations. The tusche wash was the same mixture as in Examples 7 through 12. The areas were painted in regular single strokes with a one-half-inch watercolor brush. The brush was lightly charged for each stroke, working down within the area. When dry, the crayon line was applied. It will be noticed that in each instance when the brush was removed at the end of the stroke, the deposit of tusche was much greater.

When this group of examples was completed, they appeared visually normal, and no effect of the sponge dampening was discernible. The stone was given a normal preparation. When the stone was washed out and rolled up, there was a surprise. Although a change was questioned at this stage, it was not predictable before the test. The vertical streaks showed in the washes. It should be pointed out again that at no time was any vertical stroke made except with what seemed to be a completely clean water-dampened sponge. These streaks took strength in direct proportion to the amount of tusche in the area. This observation leads one to the conclusion that any soil, caused in any manner during the gradual work on the stone, will be accentuated in the middle to dark groups.

This group of examples also indicates that even a mild resist technique can be employed successfully when a quick single application of tusche is used. This has also been found true while working tusche over dried grinding compound or dried flour paste. Many types of resists have been experimented with, and it is reasonable to state that they all have worked, providing the application of tusche is controlled. In this and other techniques discussed, unless otherwise indicated, the preparation procedure should be normal. The technique, as it is evaluated at the moment, has little or no value in itself, but is clear proof that one needs to exercise care in the development of work on the stone for even areas, and that all types of resists from the most obvious to the most subtle can be controlled. It is believed that much more may be learned from further investigation.

EXAMPLE 31

In this example a stone surface was texturally prepared before the crayon was applied. A soft stone was ground with No. 220 carborundum, and then the small blade of a very sharp pocket knife was used to lightly prepare the textural pattern in the clean surface of the stone. Some attention was given to the size of the cut, as well as to the direction and grouping. In this example

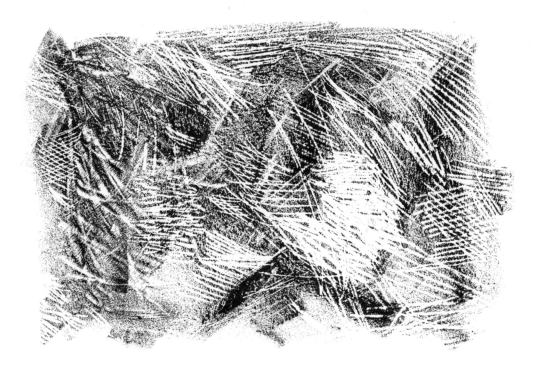

EXAMPLE 31

it was not necessary to be very precise, and the designing could be done spontaneously. However, in a part of a composition where the technique would normally be employed, it would be necessary to decide the type and quality of texture required before actual work commenced with crayon or tusche. After the knife preparation was completed, the surface was wiped with a clean cloth, and the flat side of a No. 3 Korn lithographic crayon was rubbed in a polydirectional manner over the area. Although a knife blade was used in this example, various sizes and types of cutting tools may be employed to produce different effects.

It is possible to extend this technique to include the form of the composition, as well as area texture. When it is used to establish form, an interesting effect of simultaneous positive and negative relationships can be obtained. It is advisable to caution against deep cutting because nothing is gained by depth that warrants the excessive grinding and loss of stone thickness that will be necessary to remove the textural surface for the next composition.

EXAMPLE 32

The water-tusche mixture in this example was medium dark. A heavier or lighter mixture can be used. More water would prevent range in value, and a darker mixture would print solid black. A large plastic tray was used as a tusche palette, and the mixture of tusche was brushed or flowed on the palette with a large soft-haired wash brush. Before any drying of the tusche, various sized pieces of paper were quickly rubbed or squashed onto the palette and transferred by pressing the hand or a flat surface onto the stone.

The paper used for direct transfer determines to a large extent the kind of transfer. A soft paper is absorbent and will produce an entirely different effect than a hard paper. Any type of material that will hold tusche will work. Experimentation should be done with different types of paper or other types of material, and it will be found that the weight, softness, and texture will play a direct role in the kind of transfer.

EXAMPLE 32

EXAMPLE 33

Any type of brush can be used for painting in a dry-brush manner. There is a slightly misleading connotation to the phrase, "dry brush." Although it has that appearance, the mixture of tusche and the load in the brush needs to be sufficiently liquid to allow it to be applied to the stone. It is suggested that a medium dark mixture of tusche will behave generally better than either a light or dark. However, there are times when I allow a large brush, fully loaded with thick tusche, to almost dry solid and then use it for scrubbing techniques. This, of course, produces a somewhat different effect.

In this example a No. 10 bristle brush of the Filbert type was used. It was well loaded with the tusche mixture to be sure of a balanced mixture and then

EXAMPLE 33

worked back and forth on paper until the load was believed to be correct. At the moment that the load was considered right, the painting was done on the stone. The process was repeated until the area was finished. The load in the brush and the speed at which the painting is done are critical. If there is too much tusche in the brush, the stroke will not remain crisp and clean, and capillary action will cause the strokes to spread and combine. The painting stroke, therefore, should be very fast, with a slashing type of application. When it is desired to obtain solid blacks and to also hold fine detail on the edges, it is recommended that the first application be allowed to dry, and then the heavier inside solids be filled separately. At the wash-out and roll-up stage, it is advisable that the entire work be rubbed up with liquid asphaltum.

EXAMPLE 34

This is an interesting technique and one which I discovered by accident. Under ordinary circumstances there is an even bite of the grain of the stone against the crayon, and together they produce a controlled relationship. Because of a fondness for texture, experiments have been carried out with nongreasy materials in order to produce organic textures. The example shown is the first discovered in a series that have since been developed. In this instance, powdered resin was screened to save the slightly coarser particles, and these were sprinkled in uneven amounts, depending on the effect desired, onto the clean surface of the stone. A soft crayon, Korn No. 2, was used on the flat side. By taking a firm hold with the fingers and pressing the nails into the crayon so that it can be vigorously applied in striking blows, it is possible to produce the crayon effect of a very coarsely ground stone. This immediately extends the medium and allows various surface qualities through a single type of graining. Resin is but one of numerous materials that have been tried.

EXAMPLE 34

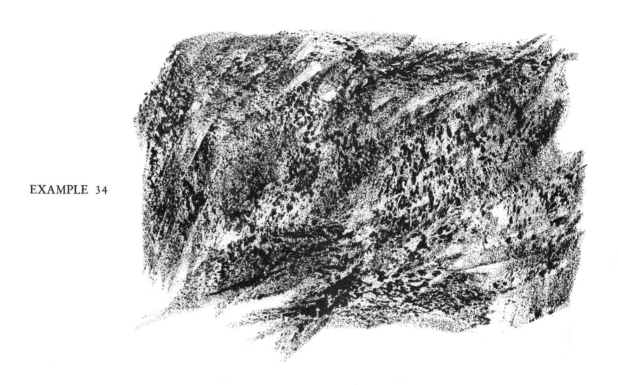

EXAMPLE 35

Turpentine tusche was used for this example. Stick tusche was dissolved into a liquid in the same manner as previously described for water tusche, except in this case turpentine was used as a diluent instead of water. For solid black work, turpentine tusche has two characteristics. It has a tendency to be fatter in a thinner amount than water tusche, and consequently it is not necessary to build it up in thickness to achieve a solid black. Also since it can be applied thinner, it works better for scraped values. With water tusche the physical thickness coagulates, becomes gummy, and prevents ease of working. In the example shown, the area was painted as a solid black and allowed to dry. Then, with a razor blade and a knife the various values were scraped out. An entire composition can be developed through the reverse method of scraping. Any grain will work, but the coarser grain has less tendency to fill. In this instance grit No. 220 was used.

It will be found that different effects can be obtained with the razor blade, depending on the angle at which it is held. Usually, in order to avoid edge cuts, the two ends of the razor blade are slightly rounded with a file. It is well to keep in mind that in lithography it is not necessary to cut deeply, in fact any deep engraving or scraping should be avoided. The medium is planographic and dependent on chemical stabilization, rather than depth of cut into the surface of the stone. All that is necessary is to expose the stone through the tusche or crayon. Although stressed before, it is worth repeating that deep cuts into the stone not only waste the stone needlessly but are difficult and time consuming to grind out.

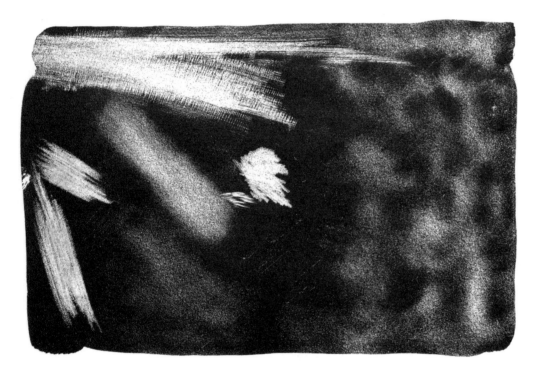

EXAMPLE 35

EXAMPLE 36

The procedure and materials were the same for this example as for the preceding one with two exceptions. The tool used on the stone to establish the lines was a sharp pocket knife. Because of the slightly convex curvature of the blade, a good pocket knife is an excellent tool for the lithographer. A diamond point was used for the fine lines. A dry point tool will work effectively but lacks the ease and flexibility of the diamond point.

One aspect to consider is that any type of cutting tool in lithography must be sharp so that a clean penetration of the grease can be made with one stroke. In general, scraped or cut lights on a ground, as indicated in this example, should be one of the last procedures during the completion of the artwork. In combined techniques it is critically important to be systematic in the development of the complete work. This does not hamper the freedom of work, and it insures that the visual decision on the stone can be held in the print.

When several types of application of crayon and tusche are intermixed back and forth, as well as other techniques, it is not possible to know with any degree of accuracy the actual amount of grease deposited into the stone. It is

EXAMPLE 36

recommended that a composition on stone be built up gradually. Within reasonable bounds, all light values of tusche are painted in first, followed by all light crayon areas, then the darks and black in tusche, ending with all heavy crayon areas. Whenever tusche is used, it should be completely dry before proceeding. If engraving or scraping is desired, it should be put in at this stage. It may be followed by any type of strong accents. Serious problems arise when these various techniques are intermixed throughout the painting or drawing of the work. No difference will be noted in the visual effects of the work on the stone. However, when the work is rolled up, areas will alter in value according to the grease deposit and this will vary greatly, depending upon the stage at which it was put on the stone.

EXAMPLE 37

EXAMPLES 37 and 38

There are several ways that a resist can be established and controlled in lithography. Most opposing materials that can be separated in vehicle and binder will work successfully. The most basic of these is accomplished with a thin gum and acid mixture. The precise effect is determined by the type of brush and technique of application. The gum arabic mixture should be as thin as possible and still maintain a slipping quality when tested with the fingers. The nitric acid

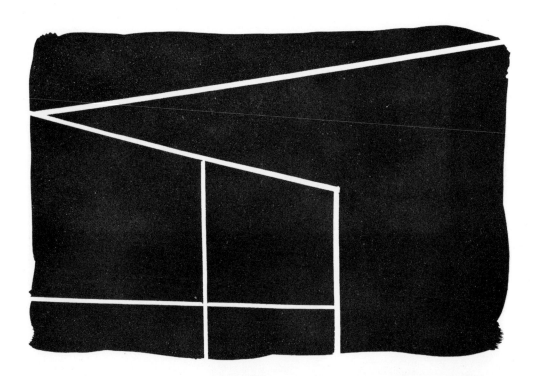

EXAMPLE 38

content should be sufficient to produce an immediate and strong effervescence when tested on the edge of the stone. With this solution pure whites are easy to establish. The area is painted with a thin coat of the gum and acid and allowed to dry. If it is desired to be able to see more fully the areas painted for resist, a small amount of powdered lampblack or dragon's blood may be mixed with the gum and acid. These substances are both inert and will not, in a small amount, alter the fixing action of the acid and gum arabic solution. When broken or semi-open areas are desired, use the dry-brush technique, as discussed in connection with Example 34. Intermixed open areas are more difficult to control; however, after a little experience, there should not be a serious problem.

After the gum arabic and acid solution has been allowed to dry thoroughly, the stone is ready to be worked with tusche or crayon. The tusche used in conjunction with this technique is always a turpentine-prepared tusche. This, in effect, separates the vehicles of the gum arabic and the tusche and allows complete freedom without dissolving either of the ingredients. Paint or draw with the assurance that the crayon or tusche will only adhere to the open stone. Although the areas that have been fixed with gum arabic and nitric acid may be covered with the tusche and crayon as the work progresses, these areas will lift off and be completely open, as previously prepared, when the work is washed out and rolled up.

EXAMPLE 39

This example belongs to the same category as Example 37. Generally, in most such cases a finely grained stone is used; in this instance, the stone was ground

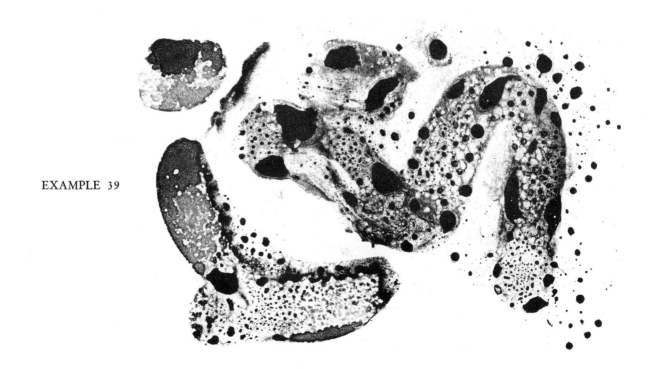

EXAMPLE 39

with 3F carborundum. The grain of the stone, however, can vary, depending on the specific work to be produced. The smaller the peaks and valleys of the grain on the stone, the finer the possible detail in the work. After the design was determined, strips of Scotch tape were securely fastened to the stone. To make even contact, these strips were rubbed with a smooth flat piece of wood through a clean piece of paper. When completed, the entire area was painted with a thick water tusche. The application of the tusche over the covered areas followed their direction and were slightly diagonal to their edge. This procedure helps to avoid underpenetration and any excess build-up of tusche on the

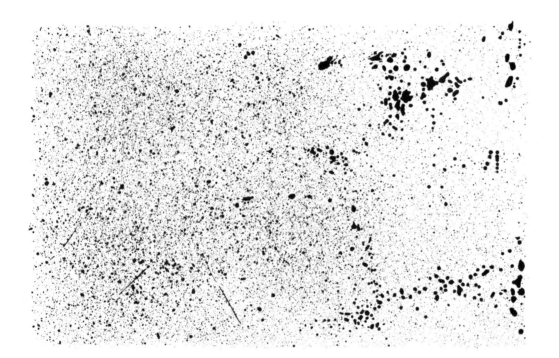

EXAMPLE 40

edges. A gummed dry wash-out is preferred to a water wash-out. There are numerous sizes and types of gummed tapes available, as well as gelatin films which give ease of control for the possibilities of this technique.

EXAMPLE 40

Examples 40 and 43 should be closely compared. The materials used were identical, and they represent two of the numerous possibilities of a mixed technique. In these examples a water-tusche mixture was used. Soft brushes work

EXAMPLE 41

better than bristle because of the light touch that must be employed. In Example 40, the areas of the design were predampened with a large brush dipped in pure turpentine; while still wet, another soft brush, filled with a medium dark mixture of water tusche, was swiftly and very lightly applied over the predampened areas of the design. Timing of the drying of the turpentine is a factor in establishing various textural possibilities. Where the turpentine is full, the larger patterns are formed, and where the turpentine is beginning to dry, the finer textures are formed. With some experience a large amount of control can be exercised over the end product. It should be emphasized that the technique demands a fresh direct once-over painting technique.

EXAMPLE 41

Spattering is produced in this instance with a medium heavy, water tusche, two small screens, a bristle brush, and a toothbrush. It will be found that, up to a point, the thicker the tusche, the finer the splatter. The finest dots were made with a one-sixteenth-inch opening screen and a No. 10 paint brush. Hold the screen at a slight angle, about eight inches from the area. Drag the bristle brush back and forth across the screen. Any area where splatter is not desired should be masked out by laying paper over it. The medium dots were made with a screen with an eighth-inch mesh. The more uneven dots in size were made by pulling a knife blade across a tusche-filled toothbrush. The heaviest dots were made after the tusche on the small screen had begun to dry. The screen was tapped with blows sharp enough to dislodge the coagulated particles of tusche. The technique is old in terms of lithography and is one that Toulouse-Lautrec used in most of his work. Many times an area in a composition needs a little extra something to break it up without a distinct brush stroke, and some form of splattering will be found extremely useful.

EXAMPLE 42

Many interesting effects of brush and finger painting can be obtained from a wipe-out method, such as seen in this example. Either water- or turpentine-prepared tusche can be used. Usually I prefer a turpentine mixture because it allows a slightly longer working time. When water tusche is used, it sticks to the area and is not so apt to allow clean free movement. This example was

EXAMPLE 42

wiped out with a finger through a thin coating of turpentine tusche. Attention is called to the detail and flow of the movement. The technique can be extended to various other manipulations using benzine and wiping with cloth, brush, or finger. It is wise, however, not to paint and wipe over an extended period of time because a thin film of transparent grease will be deposited and contrast lost. In fact, the best results are obtained when the wiping is rapid.

This method, as in some of the others discussed, is not an end in itself but an extension for subtle variations within a major handling of the medium.

EXAMPLE 43

Example 43 was painted with the same materials and equipment. The brushes, however, were thoroughly washed because each brush picks up some of both vehicles and causes coagulation. In this test the procedure was reversed, and the clear area was predampened with pure water. The evaporation and drying of water is more rapid than turpentine, but in spite of this, the working time is slightly extended when intermixed. A second brush was filled with a medium amount of water tusche, then dipped into a container of turpentine. The

EXAMPLE 43

brush was immediately applied to the predampened area. The slowness or fastness of the brush stroke and the freshness of the mixture determine the quality of texture. When applied very rapidly, small patterns are produced, and when the mixture begins to become unbalanced, more solid areas are produced. Some practice with materials and application is required to be able to control and produce desired effects.

EXAMPLE 44

EXAMPLE 44

The technique involved in Example 44 is that of engraving in lithography. The entire stone is desensitized by treating it with a medium acid and gum arabic mixture. After about six minutes of preparation with this mixture, the stone is washed clean and fanned dry. The surface of the stone is then covered with a tissue-paper-thin coat of pure gum arabic and wiped smooth with a clean cheesecloth. When the surface is dry, it is completely covered, using an ink roller well charged with black ink. To prevent the ink from coming off on the hands and smudging, a small amount of dragon's blood is rubbed into the freshly-inked surface. Sometimes French chalk is used, and this becomes a matter of preference. I happen to like the color ground better.

This procedure uses any type of cutting or engraving tool. The object is to cut through to the stone and slightly into the stone surface. Unlike metal or wood engraving, we are dealing with a chemical relationship, so there is no need to cut deeply. Again you are reminded that deep cuts should be avoided. When the engraving is completed, the visual results are reversed, and we have white lines or areas on a dark ground. Recalling at this point that we desensitized the entire stone at the beginning, the only parts that are not desensitized at present are the cut lines or areas. Take an ink roller well charged with a fat ink and roll up the work again as solid black. If it is found that rolling does not fill the engraved areas, rub the ink in with a cloth. Dust with French chalk and prepare the entire surface with a medium mixture of acid gum. Wipe the gum mixture smooth, fan dry, and wash with water. It will be found that most of the black put on the surface will wash off, leaving the engraving in reverse or as black lines or areas. Dampen the stone and wash out with turpentine. Follow the normal procedure and roll up in fairly stiff black ink. When the work is up full, dust with French chalk and give an additional mild all-over gum acid preparation. Close the stone and allow to rest for a few hours. The procedure from this point to printing is normal.

EXAMPLE 45

EXAMPLE 45

Perhaps we should discuss both types of transfer at this time, namely, gum-arabic-prepared paper and unprepared paper. There is a distinct difference between the two inasmuch as the gum-prepared paper immediately desensitizes the stone during transferring and also eliminates further additions unless the stone is counteretched. Whereas, with an unprepared paper, additional work may be carried on after the transfer has been made.

Example 45 shows the use of a gum-prepared paper transfer. Tusche in value, which incidentally is the most difficult for transfer, as well as solids and crayon, has been used. The tusche must always be a turpentine mixture in order to avoid lifting or disturbing the gum arabic. After the work is completed on the transfer paper, locate the proper position in relation to the size of the stone that will be used. A fine or medium fine grained stone will allow for greater detail. Place the stone on the press, and set the press up for printing. Cover the stone with two or three sheets of clean newsprint paper and set the pressure. Dampen the stone with water and fan dry. Dampen again and fan to mat dry. Place the transfer in position on the stone, put on the backing and pressboard, and run through the press one cycle both ways. Remove the pressure and lift up an edge of the backing to see that the transfer paper has completely adhered to the stone. Dampen the back of the transfer paper lightly with a sponge; place over this a sheet of dampened newsprint paper. Put on backing and pressboard and run through the press three or four round trips.

EXAMPLE 46.   First stage.

Remove the backing, repeat the process of dampening, and proceed with three or four additional round trips through the press. If everything has been orderly up to this point and there has not been any lost time, the transfer should be completed. If too much time is consumed in the total process, the gum on the transfer paper will dry out and stick to the stone. Assuming that everything has worked well, take two corners of the transfer paper and roll off in a back loop, exerting constant pull. If the transfer paper has dried too much and it is not possible to pull it off, dampen the back of the transfer paper sufficiently to allow removal. Gum the stone with a thin coat of pure gum arabic and fan dry. Let rest for a few minutes. Dampen the stone and remove the gum. If the stone appears to be up to the full strength, fan dry and dust with French chalk. Complete the process with a mild gum acid preparation and let rest overnight. Follow a normal procedure for printing.

EXAMPLES 46–48—Reverse Process

The example shown represents one type of reverse process. The formula is from an old source, as set forth in a French treatise. It should be noted that

EXAMPLE 47.   Second stage.

the reverse process is made possible with any combination of materials that can be separated because of a different base solvent. The basic principle involved is that at one stage what is positive or fat takes grease and subsequently is printed. Afterwards, what is negative or not fat is protected, while what is fat is washed out and resensitized. These areas are held in a sensitized form, while areas that were not fat are reversed to become positive or grease-accept-

EXAMPLE 48.   Combined with slight turn.

ing areas. In the particular method employed, the following nontested formulas were used:

1. Boil for 5 minutes, 5 cups of water with 10 grams of blonde nut gall powder. When cool, pour into a clean container. Mix 40 parts of water to 5 parts of the above mixture and 1 part of nitric acid. Hold in reserve.
2. Dissolve 5 grams of pure liquid soap in 5 cups of water, and hold in reserve.
3. In a clean container mix 5 cups of water and 2 grams of phosphoric acid and hold in reserve.
4. Mix 5 parts gum arabic solution with one part powdered lamp black and hold.

Prepare a stone as perfectly as possible. Brush the face of the stone for about one minute with formula 1, wash with clean water, and fan dry. Using formula 4, paint or draw the design, in whatever manner is desired. Registration points should be put in the margin, as for color printing. Let rest for a few hours. Take a well-charged black ink roller, and roll the work until the entire stone is solid black. Put on some water dampness with the sponge and continue to roll. It will be noticed that the work will become lighter and gradually entirely clear or in reverse of how it was painted. Fan dry and gum. Open and continue using the standard procedure for printing. Pull whatever size edition is desired. When completed, wash out and roll up in a sharp full-force condition. Proceed by painting formula 2 over the entire stone with a soft flat brush; allow to dry and repeat. When completed, fan dry, roll to a solid black with a well-charged roller, and allow to rest for 24 hours. Continue by washing the entire work with formula 3, with a light rubbing of flannel and the prepared solution. Remove all material that will come off. Wash clean with formula 3 and fan dry. Then wash with formula 1. Roll up in ink and proceed with the standard printing technique. It is noted that slight variations were found necessary. Perhaps these could have been necessary for one or a combination of several reasons: the required and nontestable humidity of the stone, the possible change in strength of materials, or faulty technique. It is advisable, therefore, to test the development in making this experiment.

For the purpose of illustration the test was successful. However, the results are slightly misleading because of the amount of work variation that was needed to produce the reverse.

In concluding this section, it should be mentioned that the technical approaches to the medium of lithography are almost endless. The intention has been in these tests and examples to suggest the basis on which to build understanding and establish a rapport with the potentials of the medium.

11

FIRST PREPARATION OF WORK

EACH phase of the work in the medium of lithography has a distinct importance to the overall quality of the end product. If the preparation of the work and stone is false in any way, the error will show up and be multiplied in the subsequent phases. An uninitiated person may feel that something has gone wrong in a latter phase, when actually the error may have been started during the preparation stage although it could not be seen. There are two basic methods for the first preparation of the work and the stone, each will be dealt with separately. The materials that are used for both types of preparation are gum arabic, French chalk, powdered resin and nitric acid. The characteristics of these materials have been described earlier. At this time we will examine their use and function.

French chalk is a very pure powder of calcium or soapstone. It is often used as a base in better face powders. This material is sprinkled over the entire surface of the finished work of the crayon and tusche on the stone. From ordinary visual appearance, not much of the powder seems to stick. However, under a powerful magnifying glass it can be seen that a small amount has adhered to the entire work surface of crayon and tusche. The chalk is applied with a powder puff or clean cloth, and the excess is removed with the fatty base of the forearm. French chalk has the function of protecting or fortifying the crayon and tusche from the possibility of too much corrosive action of either the acid or gum. It is primarily a protecting agent.

Powdered resin is sprinkled on next, in the same manner as the chalk, and wiped across the face of the stone over the worked and the unworked areas. Then, as before, the excess is removed but not wiped clean. In the future one may at some time forget to put the powdered resin on the stone. If so, it will immediately be noticed that the gum curls up, will not stick smoothly, becomes spotty, and curls into small puddles. No real damage will be done because of this oversight unless the stone is left open. In an instance such as this, immediately cup off the excess gum with the hand and place a piece of clean newsprint paper over the entire face of the work, thereby closing the stone. This keeps the air away from the edges of the puddles and prevents a corrosive action. The main purpose of the powdered resin is to create a bond between the stone and the gum arabic.

Chemically pure nitric acid is a strong and very corrosive acid with two functions to perform. It is a cleaning agent for removing any type of greasy dirt or invisible smears of grease that have accidentally collected on the open parts of the work. The most important function of nitric acid is as a helping agent in stimulating and releasing gases for the combined chemical reaction between all ingredients. The amount of acid used is in drops or is determined by the visual reactions on the stone.

Of the materials used during this phase of the work, gum arabic is the most important. Gum arabic is purchased in lump, crystal, powdered, or liquid form. Each will work as effectively as the other, the lump being the cheapest of the four. If the gum is used or purchased in liquid form, then nothing further need be done to it. However, if it is any of the other forms, it must be dissolved in water. This is done by taking approximately a double handful of gum arabic, placing it in a jar, and covering it with water. Stir it occasionally and let it stand until completely dissolved. The gum arabic will absorb more than its bulk of water, so additional water may need to be added. Before it is used, test it for consistency. It should be about as heavy as maple syrup but not as heavy as molasses. If the gum arabic is too thick, it will not be absorbed into the stone, and the calcification or hardening of the stone cannot properly take place. If, on the other hand, it is too thin because of excess water, the chemical action will not take place because of too little gum arabic. It is well to keep in mind that the gum arabic should be about the consistency of heavy maple syrup. The best way of testing is by putting the finger and thumb into the liquid and pinching the finger and thumb together as if one were snapping the fingers. If the fingers continue to slip, the gum is in good condition, but if it dries out and one is able to squeeze through the gum arabic, this indicates that the gum is too thin. Gum arabic is the principal material around which all other materials act as helping agents in making a lithograph.

We are now ready to prepare the work and the stone. The first approach discussed is basic for preparation and should be considered essential to any other. Place the stone on the gumming table, dust it with French chalk and powdered resin, and remove the excess (Figs. 20-23). In a small bowl place approximately one-half cup dissolved gum arabic, and into this put eight drops of nitric acid. Test this mixture on the edge of the stone to determine the amount of action. If there immediately is a strong frothing, there is too much nitric acid, and slightly more gum arabic should be added. Continue to test until the mixture, when tested, produces a mild slow action—not abrupt or spontaneous. The amount of acid varies, depending on the viscosity of the gum, the

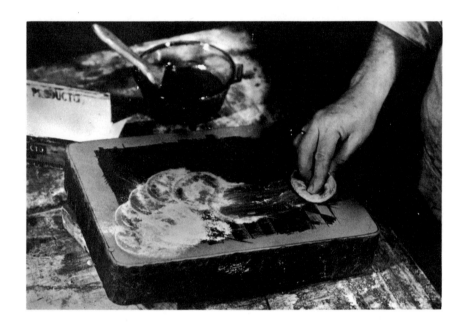

Figure 20   Putting on French chalk.

character of the work, the softness of the stone, and the temperature. When this solution has been established, pour a quantity on the face of the work on the stone. Move it around gently with a sponge or your hand, keeping it in motion for about three minutes. At the end of this time, remove the excess gum with the hand into the original bowl of gum acid. The hand cupped and moved laterally is an excellent method of removing the excess gum. Remix the ingredients, pour back onto the work, and repeat the performance for approximately the same length of time. When completed, cup off the gum acid into the acid bowl and flatten out the ridges of the gum remaining on the stone.

Put the stone in the rack to rest, preferably for overnight. Under unusual or forced conditions it is possible to go to the next phase of preparation for printing within three or four hours. This is not recommended because there is a time element involved here quite similar to other experiences where ingredients take time to merge and become fixed. With this in mind it is understood that the resting is assuring a cleaner edition of printing than would otherwise be possible. It is recommended that one become thoroughly proficient with the handling of the first basic method of preparation before proceeding to the second. This is stressed because it is easier to make an error in judgment in the second method.

The described approach to the formation of the mixture of acid and gum is important. It is contrary to the method of an exact measured amount of gum and acid. Experience with the so-called "exact" formula has proved that it is not exact, and without scientific instruments it can never be exact except by accident.

There are many items that cannot be measured or controlled under ordinary studio working conditions. A few of these are the weather, time of the year, room temperature, amount of humidity, and precise thickness of the gum. The list could continue for some time. To describe a situation that existed on two consecutive days this summer should be sufficient proof. On the first day referred to the outdoor temperature was 92 degrees, and it was very dry. The rolling of a damp stone allowed only four seconds before drying. Fanning the stone dried it almost immediately. The following day the temperature had dropped to 70 degrees, and the air was filled with moisture. It was almost impossible to roll the stone dry, and it took three or four minutes to fan the stone dry. It is no exaggeration to state that such conditions represent only part of a cross section of conditions during a working year. Heat accelerates the action and affects the amount of material used. Cold and moisture retard action. These are prime factors in determining the action of the preparation of materials. Although materials are always stated in amount and measurements, the final and accurate test is the analysis of the action. For the reasons indicated, it will be assumed henceforth, as far as this treatise is concerned, that judgment and observation are the means of determining the result.

The second method for first preparation of the work and stone is based essentially upon the method just discussed, except that this time the procedure is broken down into gradual steps. Place the stone on the gumming rack and prepare as before. Take a bowl and put into it one cup of gum arabic and eight drops of nitric acid. This mixture of nitric acid will not show a reaction on the stone; therefore, it is necessary to start each time with fresh gum and a measured amount of acid. Since with this mixture there is no visual way of determining the reaction, it is important that the artist have experience with

Figure 21. Dusting with powdered resin.

the basic method of preparation and that this process be attempted for the first time under normal temperature and humidity conditions. Apply the solution with a small watercolor brush, about a No. 6. Brush this on the darker areas of the work, both the darkest crayon and darkest tusche. Go over these areas with a fresh mixture approximately twice and then begin to radiate out from these areas to other slightly lighter areas. Gradually continue this procedure until everything, with the exception of the very lightest areas, has been gummed. At this point take a clean sponge or your hand and spread what is on the stone over the entire work, including all the light grays. There is enough strength remaining in what is on the stone, although slightly worn out, to fix the lightest grays without disturbing them. Wipe the excess off the stone with

Figure 22. Removing excess of chalk and resin.

Figure 23. Overall gumming.

the sponge or hand, and repeat the same procedure. Commencing with the darkest darks and gradually radiating out to the lighter darks and medium grays until you have completed a second cycle. It is recommended that the procedure be repeated three times. When completed, the stone should rest for a period of twelve hours. It may rest up to twenty-four hours.

It has been observed that a very small amount of nitric acid is employed in this method. Instead of a direct fixing of the stone and work as in the first method, it is necessary to accomplish the same overall effect by more and longer applications of the weaker solution. It is also necessary to carry this second method of preparation over into the roll-up and wash-out phase. Particular attention will be called to it during that discussion. There are other methods of preparing the stone and work which are not mentioned because they are neither basic nor essential and could be confusing. Under the chapter on Methods and Special Techniques, a direct-acid method will be discussed.

Emil Weddige
"An Angel Passed This Night"
edition 50
25¾" x 19¾" (horizontal)

25/50   An angel passed this night   Enid W. eldre

12

WASH-OUT AND ROLL-UP

THERE are also two distinctly different technical methods of procedure for the wash-out and roll-up phase. It would be difficult to state which one is better; each has advantages. Occasionally one is better suited to a particular problem. In general, the method used is a question of preference. It is suggested that we commence with the wet method because it presents fewer problems.

The wash-out and roll-up phase requires that we use all the equipment and materials of printing with the exception of the press for printing. I prefer to do the work on the press, so that if for any reason during the process a proof needs to be pulled, the work is in a relative position to do so. Check all equipment. Place the stone on the bed of the press. Take a leather ink roller and scrape it with an ordinary table knife. The knife should have a rounded edge so that it is not sharp. Scrape the dead ink off the roller, as shown in Fig. 24. Place a small fresh supply of ink on the ink table and break it down with the ink knife. Rolling-up black is good for this phase; however, any available black ink, when properly balanced, will do just as well. The mixing brings it to room temperature and also makes it malleable to its normal consistency. Add a small amount of No. 470 oil, and mix in thoroughly. When the ink is of the proper consistency for use, it will slightly flatten out when put into a single pile. If there is too much oil, it will appear soupy and flatten immediately. If there is not enough oil, it will remain in its position as a heavy angular mass. It will be

Figure 24. Proper scraping of roller.

necessary to experiment with ink mixing until the proper consistency is arrived at (Fig. 25). Keep in mind that it is desirable to have the ink in balance, in terms of grease, with the work that has been put on the stone. It may be advisable at this time to review the chapter on Ink and Related Materials. The roll-up should be with a very stiff tacky ink, which is slightly more tacky than if one were in the process of printing. We are facing the work for the first time in transfer from crayon and tusche to ink, and we do not want the work to roll up or take ink rapidly or deposit more grease than was originally intended with the crayon and tusche.

Place a small amount of the prepared ink on the rolling part of the ink slab, and roll out with the ink roller. Roll back and forth for two or three minutes,

Figure 25. Layout of ink table.

Figure 26.   Charging the ink table.

turning the ink roller end to end, so as to make an even charge of ink over the entire roller (Figs. 26 and 27). When this is completed, rest the ink roller in the rack and proceed to check other materials.

It is necessary to have on hand a small brush about one-fourth inch in diameter, two clean water sponges, a small gum sponge, a bowl with about one cup of clean gum arabic, and a bottle of nitric acid, plus one or two clean cloths. It should be mentioned that it is a mistake to start the wash-out and roll-up phase and then to find that you have not checked these supplies, because once

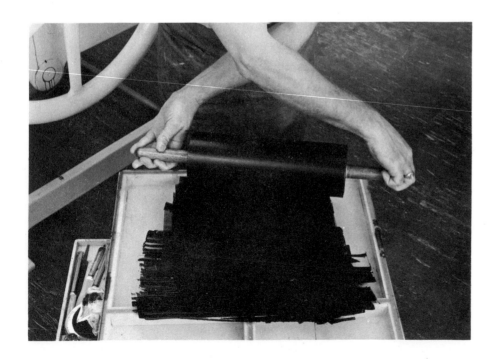

Figure 27.   Flattening the ink.

the stone is opened, the process should continue without interruption. Recall at this time what has been previously stated—that the principle of lithography is based upon the premise of the separation between water and grease.

With the equipment in order, proceed with the wet method of wash-out and roll-up. Take a clean sponge and wash the face of the stone thoroughly with water. Do not scrub or use pressure but rinse many times until every aspect of the dried gum arabic has been removed from both the stone and the work. When the washing is completed, use a hand fan to fan the stone dry (Fig. 28). Follow by flooding the stone with water. It may seem peculiar to fan dry and

Figure 28. Mr. Gary Shepperdson helps in preparation.

then immediately wet the stone. There are two reasons for this procedure. It creates a greater suction of moisture into the face of the stone and helps to make a better separation between the artwork and the open stone. The second reason is based on the principle of cooling through evaporation. Proceed by flooding the stone with water. It is not necessary to flood the floor or the bed of the press, but it is important that there is an abundance of water over the entire face of the stone. On top of the water immediately sprinkle about one tablespoon of turpentine, and with one of the clean cloths gently wash out the crayon and tusche. Move fairly rapidly without any scrubbing pressure until all of the crayon and tusche is melted (Fig. 29). You may be able to do this in one operation. If you should find from the appearance of the stone that it is beginning to show indications of drying, stop immediately. Take a clean sponge and remove all accumulated sludge. Rinse the sponges, wipe the stone clean, reflood the stone, and add more turpentine; continue the process until every indication of crayon and tusche has been removed. Wipe the stone clean and fan dry. As the work dries, you will notice that there is a ghost of the work that was put on the stone. This ghost is caused by the transparent grease content that has been embedded into the face of the stone.

When the stone is dry, redampen with a clean, slightly wet sponge. Try to dampen the stone evenly and avoid, at this phase, any excess water. To dampen

Figure 29. Beginning wash-out.

means that there is moisture in the face of the stone but not noticeably on it. Excess water will be picked up by the ink roller, and it will be impossible to ink the work evenly. Study the accompanying diagram of Fig. 30 and establish a method of dampening the stone that is not varied from one time to the next. Keep in mind that it is easy to wet the stone, but the requirement for dampening is to deposit precisely the same amount of moisture each time. This cannot be a swish here or there. Only the same amount of moisture and the same amount of ink will produce the same quality of print.

Pick up the ink roller and recharge it on the ink slab. Dampen the work again. Immediately pass the ink roller back and forth over the face of the work.

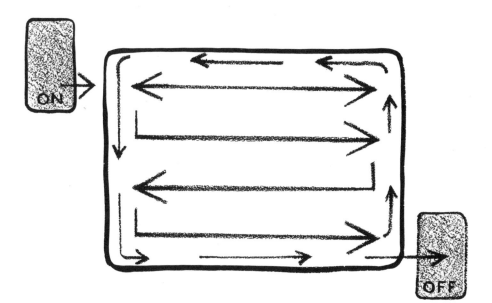

Figure 30. *Dampening the stone.*

Study the method and manner in which the ink roller fits the various locations of light and dark in the work. It is necessary with each new work to determine how it can best be rolled. During the roll-up one learns how to roll the particular stone to obtain the best results for printing the edition (Fig. 31). Make four or five passes with the ink roller, watching the surface to see that there is no drying. Put the ink roller on the ink slab. Dampen the face of the work and recharge the roller. Dampen the work again and follow with another inking.

Continue this cycle until the artwork on the stone comes up to full force. It is desirable that the work should not grab or come up fast. Instead it should come

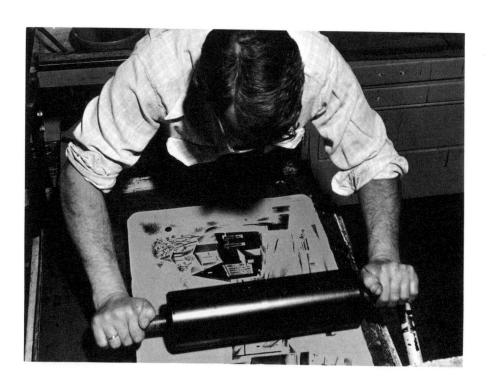

Figure 31. *Roll-up.*

up slowly to full strength. When the work appears precisely the same as it was painted or drawn, fan the work dry. Dust the work with French chalk and powdered resin and remove the excess. Put on a tissue-paper-thin layer of pure gum arabic, evenly over the entire stone. Place the work in the rack, and allow it to rest for four to six hours.

The second method of wash-out and roll-up is the dry gum method. Under the dry gum method everything that has been said about the preparation of materials remains the same. Here most of the similarity stops. The first step is to remove the old gum that was left on the stone after the first preparation. With a damp sponge, very slowly and carefully dissolve the old gum. Wipe the stone and work as clean as possible. Avoid any pressure in cleaning because in the dry gum method none of the artwork should dissolve. If a slight amount of crayon or tusche dissolves, one need not be too concerned. However, if a quantity dissolves as sometimes happens when the crayon or tusche is physically thick and should dark areas wash out light, discontinue the dry gum method of wash-out and immediately revert to the wet method. If the old gum washes off without excess loss of crayon or tusche, proceed with the dry gum method and fan the stone dry. Cover the stone with a tissue-paper-thin coat of pure gum arabic. Work the gum sponge horizontally and diagonally back and forth to be sure that the entire work and stone has been covered with gum. Fan the stone dry. When it is positively dry, we are ready to proceed. A word of caution here is important. Keep water, damp sponges, damp rags, or damp hands completely away from the stone during this phase of the dry gum wash-out and roll-up. Sprinkle about one tablespoon of turpentine on the dry gummed stone. Take a dry clean cloth and wash out the crayon and tusche. Avoid scrubbing; a light, dissolving type of action is desirable.

When the artwork has been completely removed with turpentine and the sludge removed with clean dry cloths, there are three possible choices of procedure. First, a rub-up may be done with a small amount of ink and turpentine on a clean cloth. This helps to bring the inking up more quickly. Or, second, a small amount of liquid asphaltum on a cloth may be rubbed into the face of the work. Some lithographers use an asphaltum rub-up as a common practice. It is not recommended, however, because liquid asphaltum will build up extra grease, and about fifty percent of the time this is not desirable. It is recommended that a liquid asphaltum rub-up be used only when it has been determined that the work is lean. It should be understood that if either rub-up method is used proceed with it while the stone is covered with the thin coat of gum arabic. The third possible procedure is to eliminate any form of rub-up and proceed directly to rolling the work up in ink. With each method the gum arabic is removed with a water-dampened sponge, fanned dry, and redampened prior to rolling up in ink. Stop inking when the artwork seems sharp and up to the degree it appeared originally.

When the work is brought up to full force, fan dry and close the stone with a thin coat of pure gum. Allow the stone to rest from four to six hours.

It is necessary at this time to backtrack and refer to the second method of First Preparation of Work. After the work is fanned dry, as described in the preceding paragraph, it is possible to complete the procedure by the second method of preparation, explained in Chapter 11.

Take a weak solution of gum arabic and nitric acid; although this solution is still considered weak, it is about twice as strong as that originally described in First Preparation of Work and Stone. Add about eight drops of nitric acid to one-half cup of gum arabic and mix thoroughly. It will be noticed that when this solution is applied to the work, there is a slight reaction. Paint this solution of gum arabic and nitric acid on with a small brush, over the darker areas of the artwork, and proceed in the same manner as previously described. This cycle is completed twice for a period of perhaps three minutes each. Wipe the entire face of the stone with a clean sponge at the completion of each cycle of the process. When finished, wipe the stone clean and fan dry. Put on a thin coat of pure gum and fan dry. The stone is now ready to be put into the rack to rest for four to six hours.

It is mentioned here that the time may come when, at this particular stage of the work, it will seem desirable to proof the work on newsprint paper. If this is the case, the stone should be set up on the press, as described in Chapter 13, and a dry newsprint proof pulled. Proofing should not be done merely because one is anxious to see a proof. If the work has been uneven or spotty in rolling up, or if areas of the work have not taken ink, it is advisable to pull a newsprint proof to determine if fatter ink is necessary to bring the work up to full force. Conversely, if there are no questions about the artwork and it has come up full, a trial proof at this time is not recommended because there is the danger of having a good preparation become too greasy.

Emil Weddige
"Pax vo Bis"
edition 12
22½" x 30" (vertical)

13

PRINTING IN BLACK AND WHITE

ON the day of printing, the first thing to do is to check all equipment that is used in printing. Lay out the worktable spaces, so that it is possible to rotate clockwise or counterclockwise around the press, whichever is more convenient (Fig. 32). The ink slab should be about a step or a step and a half from the open or front end of the press. The press should be checked to see that everything is in working condition. A fresh supply of the materials used during the wash-out and roll-up should be on hand. The stone is placed upon the bed of the press and centered both end-to-end and back-to-front. A scraper is selected that will cover the entire face of the work and yet not be wider than the stone (Fig. 33). It is checked to see that it is smooth and then placed in the scraper slot and tightened with the thumbscrew. The pressboard is checked for size. In all instances the pressboard must be at least slightly larger than the printing paper and larger than the stone. Put a thin film of lard or pressboard grease on the pressboard and on the scraper leather.

Have a selection of backing ready; old proofs are generally used for this purpose. Also, have on hand a stack of newsprint paper. One word of economy about newsprint paper. It is the cheapest material that is used, and one can consider it inexpensive. It is not inexpensive, however, if it is wasted; in fact, it can be the most expensive item in the studio budget. After it is dry, it can be used over again, so stack it in a clean area and rotate the total supply. Much of the newsprint paper that I am using in my studio has been used for several

Figure 32.   Relation of equipment.

years. The amount of newsprint should be well in excess of the number of prints that are expected to be pulled.

The sheets of printing paper for the total edition should be at the head of the paper arrangement, so that they are handy to the press and preferably to the left of the ink slab. The rotation is—from clean paper—to ink slab—to press—to backing and pressboard—to the stack of finished proofs. At this point it is wise to be sure that there is a fresh supply of mixed gum on hand, in case it is needed. Check the exact place where the scraper is to start and stop, and mark the press with chalk (Fig. 34). Proceed with a wash-out and roll-up, as discussed in detail in the preceding chapter.

Figure 33.   Marking of press and relation of scraper.

Figure 34.   *Start and stop of pull.*

When arriving at the point where the work is up to full force, set the pressure on the press. The pressure is set by placing a piece of newsprint on the inked stone, then the backing on top, and finally the pressboard over the backing (Figs. 34 and 35). Push the bed of the press under the head of the scraper, up to the point where it is marked on the bed of the press for starting. Pull the pressure lever down to about ten o'clock or to the crotch of the arm and hold it there by leaning against it (Fig. 36). Screw the turnscrew at the top of the press down until you feel contact between the scraper and the pressboard. By trial and error, adjust the pressure to the point where it seeems like you are pulling or lifting about 70 to 90 pounds. If you have never lifted this amount of weight, put on the amount of pressure that seems reasonable but not exces-

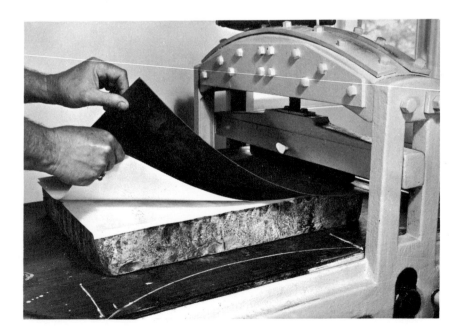

Figure 35.   *Relation of paper and backing.*

sive in relation to your strength. The clearness of the proof will immediately indicate if the pressure is correct. Check Figs. 36 and 37 to see the position of the arms and body for exercising the proper leverage. From the 70 to 90 pound pull, the press is built to produce 6000 to 8000 pounds pressure per square inch on the stone from the scraper. In some instances this amount is increased to approximately 10,000 pounds, depending on the roughness, thickness, and dryness of the paper. At first it will seem difficult to put on the pressure, but as soon as one acquires the correct position for leverage, it will not require a great effort. Put the pressure handle down as far as it will go and crank the bed through to the other chalk mark where the artwork ends (Fig. 35). Take the

Figure 36. Relation of pressure lever and crank.

pressure off, and pull the bed back. Remove separately the assembly of pressboard, backing, and print. Dampen the stone with water immediately.

As time goes on there will be established a rhythm for rolling, printing, and dampening, so that this time factor does not vary a great deal. It must be remembered that once the gum has been washed off, the stone is open to the air and should have a constant dampness in order to keep the work in proper balance. The work will gain or lose depending to an extent on the evenness of the dampness.

It is advisable to pull several proofs on newsprint paper. Bring the work up to full force on this inexpensive and rather smooth-surfaced paper. When every-

Figure 37. Pulling a proof.

thing is working well, pull a proof on good paper. In spite of the fact that several proofs have been pulled, it will be found that the first proof on good paper is generally light. This is the time when slightly more pressure is put on the press, and the ink roller is made a little richer with fresh ink. The reason for this adjustment is that the good paper is softer and has a greater tooth than the newsprint paper. Actually the change to good paper is an insurance against the risk of overcharging the work with ink. After the adjustment has been made, pull another proof on good paper. If by the third good-paper proof the work is not up to full, clear form, then, according to the discussion on inks, critically examine the condition of the ink. Adjust the ink if necessary and proceed.

Figure 38. Lifting weight of roller with thumbs.

When the proofing is full and is precisely what had been anticipated through the work on the stone, mark this proof to indicate that it is the standard for the edition. The classic manner is to label it *bon tirage,* or if a less classical indication is preferred, mark it *proof for edition.* This proof should be put on a bulletin board in front of the press where it can be constantly referred to throughout the edition. If it is necessary to stop printing for any reason before the edition is completed, ink the work, close it with a thin layer of gum, and fan dry. When work is resumed, wipe off the gum with a damp sponge and pull a newsprint proof. Thereafter continue with the edition.

Let us assume that difficulties develop during the course of printing and that it is found that certain areas are either becoming cloudy or have a tendency to fill. The old adage that an ounce of prevention is worth a pound of cure is certainly most applicable in all such situations in lithography. As recommended, the condition of the print is constantly observed in relation to the *bon tirage.* If there is any change, even the slightest, that is the time to make all necessary corrections or adjustments. It is unwise to wishfully hope that the damage will not increase. It will, most surely, become worse in a very short time, and the work can become solid black, nonrepairable, and be lost completely. A gradual increase in excess fat or grease is like a prairie fire that is slow to start but once started is almost impossible to stop. If for any reason the work clouds or begins to fill, it is recommended that the work be fanned dry. Follow with a complete wash-out and roll-up. When the work is back up to full force, give it a coat of mild acid gum and fan dry. After a few minutes rest, wash the gum off, and proceed with the printing. Pay particular attention to the cloudy area in rolling. Under more difficult situations when it may be necessary to perform a second wash-out and roll-up, use the same procedure, but stop printing and rest the stone overnight.[1] There are times when an experienced lithographer can apply a very mild etch without going through a wash-out. This is not recommended for the beginner, but keep it in mind for later reference.

When the printing of the edition is completed and the count has been verified, the stone should be canceled. There are several ways that work may be canceled. Generally, it is done with some turpentine on a rag wiped through the work, or with a razor blade scraped through the work. A proof is then pulled to show that the stone has been canceled. This proof is marked *artist's canceled proof.* It is signed, dated, and will serve to prove that the edition was completed and that the artist supervised the canceling.

---

[1] See "When the Work Darkens," page 194.

Emil Weddige
"Landscape Valencia"
edition 40
19¾" x 13" (horizontal)

14

METHODS AND SPECIAL TECHNIQUES

THROUGHOUT this work an attempt has been made to establish a critical viewpoint and a pragmatic approach to the solving of problems. The possible variations of work and solutions are so numerous that one could consider them as inexhaustible. Because of this, the serious student of lithography has to become an inventor, as well as an explorer. The basic general approach has been discussed. Some special variations, along with other methods, are detailed in this chapter. The reader is reminded that the writer, like all experienced persons, naturally has preferred methods and techniques. In spite of this and anything that may have been interpreted otherwise, I firmly believe that any technique or procedure that has been proven in use is a good way to work. Furthermore, the growth and development of the medium will be fostered by searching out new answers.

After the general approach to the various stages of lithography, a very brief time should be allowed for the analysis of problems which may develop, since it is necessary to solve these problems by putting secondary procedures into operation at the instant of need. Some general studio procedures and special techniques follow.

STORAGE OF WORK

When work is in progress, no special preparation for storage is necessary. If one stops printing before the edition is completed, even for a rest break, the work should be gummed. However, when work is to be set aside for an extended period of time, from a few weeks to a longer period, it is desirable and sometimes mandatory that the work be covered more securely with gum arabic. After the work is rolled up sharp, gum the stone a little fuller than usual, and while the gum is moist, cement a piece of clean newsprint paper over the face. This helps to prevent the ink from drying, and it also prevents any oxygen from the air burning through the gum into the face of the stone. There are occasions when work is stored for a period of years. Under such abnormal situations of storage, it is recommended that every six months the work be washed out and rolled up in fresh ink and again prepared for long-term storage. Otherwise, the gums, varnishes, and oils in the ink will dry out, crystallize, and flake off. Unless re-inked, the grease in the stone will dry out, and the work could be lost.

CHOICE OF GRAIN OF STONE

Although this subject has been discussed on two previous occasions, a few words more on the topic might be advisable. The grain is always selected in relation to the type of work that is to be done. In color, where one has a group of stones to be painted, the surface should be selected as to coarseness or fineness in terms of the character of the work. For example, on a stone to receive a large amount of crayon and crayon texture, it would be desirable to have a coarser grain, such as 180 or 220, whereas with a stone where a wash or tusche is to be used, it would be desirable to have a 1F or 2F graining. An extremely detailed fine stone that might include pen lines or extremely fine engraving would undoubtedly require a 3F grain.

There is another aspect related to color that should be considered. In an edition, for example, of five stones or five colors, if each stone was grained the same, there would be a tendency for the finished character of the work to have a solid or filled appearance because of the repeated grain. The difference in grain between two colors in overlay enhances the effect of color and helps greatly to produce a translucent quality.

REGRAINING A PART OF THE STONE

In addition to using stones with different graining, there are two other possibilities, one of which is the regraining of a particular area. The work may have gone through the entire process up to the point of proofing, and at this time it is decided that one of the areas is unsatisfactory or has become damaged. If there were no other way to resolve the problem, it would be necessary to discard the stone and start over. However, it is possible in such a case to regrain a part of the stone. Open the entire stone and wash down thoroughly, removing every trace of gum. Keep the entire stone damp throughout the process of area regraining. Take a small piece of broken limestone, about three inches in size, and the same type of grinding compound that was originally used, and with these grind out and regrain the part to be corrected. Use the same technique on a minor scale that is employed for ordinary graining. One should study the composition so as to follow a natural separation in the work without particularly forming a straight line unless there is a definite break in the composition that would permit this. Follow the regraining process for what would amount to three grindings, and then wash the stone and fan dry. As soon as it is dry, regum very thinly the parts of the composition that have been retained to within one-half inch from the newly grained area. Fan dry and proceed with the artwork on the newly sensitized area. When completed, prepare the entire stone by standard procedure, as if it were a totally new work.

The second possibility for area graining is to produce a variety of textures. If used, it is one that is practiced at the original graining period. There are interesting effects that may be obtained by this procedure. Nothing demands that the entire stone be grained in any particular fashion, and it is reasonable, therefore, to make the grain of one area of the stone with extremely coarse No. 80 grit for example, another area of the stone with No. 220 grit, and still another area of the stone with No. 1F grit. This textural variety can be extremely interesting when seen in the finished print.

BREAKING IN A NEW ROLLER

The process of breaking in a new ink roller forces me to admit that it is far better to purchase a leather ink roller that has been broken in and pay the small additional fee than it is to attempt to break one in. An ink roller actually improves with age. This is relative, of course, up to a point. An ink roller normally used and taken care of properly should last about ten or fifteen years. It takes approximately one month under normal circumstances to break in an ink roller. I have found that this is one of those jobs in which students have no particular interest. As a result the problem can become difficult, because if the roller is not thoroughly scraped down regularly, the leather will take the ink unevenly and become spotty. Once hard spots are formed, they are practically impossible to remove. On the other hand, if a roller has been rolled up very fat each day and scraped down after a few rollings, it eventually will become a very sensitive tool to use.

The breaking-in procedure recommended is quite simple. Take a quantity of left-over ink that has been made too fat for printing by the addition of linseed oil. Roll the ink roller on the slab in this mixture two or three times whenever passing by the slab. At the close of the day take an ordinary inexpensive table knife that has had the edge honed round so that it is not sharp, and scrape the roller hard. In fact one cannot scrape it too hard if the knife edge is dull.

I generally put one handle of the ink roller against the bed of the press and lean my stomach against the other end. Use both hands to hold the knife at right angles to the roller, and scrape the roller from end to end. Put the scrapings on a piece of paper or preferably the center of the roller (see Fig. 21). When the circumference has been scraped, remove the ink from the center and scrape both ends with a circular motion. The roller now should be loaded with a fat ink and placed in the rack. The next day, or at the next opportunity, follow the same procedure. Whenever the studio is left for a vacation or an extended period of time, it is recommended that the ink roller be wrapped in wax paper or plastic material to prevent any excess drying. Composition rollers are fine for certain things, but a good leather roller is a pleasure to use.

ADVANTAGES AND DISADVANTAGES OF DAMP PAPER

Much can be said regarding printing with damp or dry paper; suffice it here to merely make a few comments on the subject. The simplest way to dampen paper is lightly to pass a sponge fully loaded with water over each side of the paper, first horizontally on one side and then vertically on the other. It is best to work rapidly so as not to allow time for the paper to buckle. When dampened, double wrap the stack of paper in a sheet of polyethylene, of the type that can be purchased at a lumber yard. When the paper is wrapped, flip the package on a flat surface with a sharp slap, this will completely flatten the paper and remove air pockets. It is advisable to dampen the paper the night before it is to be used. Do not allow it to remain wrapped for longer than forty-eight hours.

When printing on damp paper in black and white, there is a beautiful rapport between the work, the ink, and the paper. The damp paper, no matter how thick or how rough, will press into exact contact with the work and produce the highest quality of printing throughout the edition. There is no question in my mind that printing with damp paper has decided advantages. It allows for a free choice in type of paper and eliminates the need for extreme pressure on the press. Also dampened paper has the distinct advantage of keeping the stone constantly moist during the actual time of printing. This protects the work throughout the edition, whereas with dry paper the stone always drys out during the seconds that are involved in printing, and this is often the cause for the filling or darkening of the work. When one prints dry, there is a much greater tendency to overink with a consequent loss of the delicate relationships that distinguish a quality lithograph.

There is one distinct disadvantage in using dampened paper. It has a tendency to buckle in drying and needs to be dried in a flat book or paper press. A flat book consists of layers of large cardboard, beaverboard, or homosote in which the edition is placed immediately after printing, while the paper is still slightly damp. Many lithographers find the buckling of the paper such a distinct disadvantage that they would prefer the use of dry paper, in order to avoid the need to flatten the finished edition. A compromise may be made with paper in order to avoid dampening it by preflattening before the actual printing. This is done by using a sheet of good paper as the first sheet of backing, then alternating throughout the edition with the preflattened paper next as the printed paper and a new sheet of good paper as the first sheet of backing. This method does help to smooth the paper and makes for better contact with the surface of the print.

In colorwork, unless one has a scientifically-controlled moisture box, it is impossible to print on dampened paper. This is because of the concern with registration. If dampened paper is used but is not dampened to the same degree, the paper will stretch unevenly and consequently any type of registration would be lost. In order to use a rough paper in colorwork, I have, on occasion, used a dampened paper on the first stone, and then set the registration points after this has been printed. It is normally recommended that a good quality of fairly smooth surfaced paper be used for all colorwork. This eliminates many of the problems. Regardless of whether dry or damp paper is used for printing, it is necessary to face and resolve certain problems and limitations of each.

RESTORATION

In connection with papers, it may be of some interest that recently I worked on the restoration of prints that had been in a fire at the Arwin Gallery, Detroit, Michigan, on December 18, 1963. Approximately 400 prints were involved, and their value was beyond my mathematics. The damage was devastating, and the situation was reminiscent of an old barn raising when the neighbors all pitched in to help a friend restore his barn after a fire. My past experience in making paper gave me some knowledge of the problems involved in restoration.

An immediate check was made with Dr. R. W. Parry of The University of Michigan, a chemist whose knowledge of the effects of various chemicals in relation to paper content was generously given. Fortified with several materials but with a great amount of apprehension, I set up a temporary workshop. A study was made of a cross section of the various types of damage. A proof print of my own work was soiled as an example of the overall damage involved; the damages included: water mixed with dirt and fire-extinguisher chemicals had caused streaks; soil mixed with either of the above had stained as with a dye; color that was water solvent had run and streaked; there were boot and shoe marks, rust marks, and, in addition, there was a quantity of grease deposited from various equipment and building materials. The floor had been flooded with water and the following day had been a solid cake of ice with everything fastened together. In some instances, overzealous attempts at separating layers of prints had caused parts of one print to adhere to another. Luckily this had not happened often, because it presented a peculiar jigsaw puzzle to fit the correct pieces in their proper places. Rust stains were bizarre; in one instance the only blemish was a soiled red image of a No. 8 common nail that stained the paper on both sides and appeared as clearly as if it had been photographed.

It was learned that the best procedure for restoration was to do one thing at a time and to work from the obvious to the complex. All prints were cleaned of dry surface dirt and separated into piles of common damage. The cleaning then followed a sequence of: grease, rust, color dye, rust dye, and waterstain. Ninety-five percent of all of the prints had buckled from the water and needed to be flattened. This was done with an electric iron set at a temperature for silk and using a fresh sheet of water-dampened newsprint paper on the surface of the print. It should be noted that direct heat will set most types of stain and that it is important to have the work completely restored before using heat. Personal danger can result from the mixture of the various chemicals and the gases given off, so details of the process will be reported in a separate article. One aspect that was constantly clear was that the quality of the paper determined the potential for complete restoration. The knowledge acquired during the project may be helpful in similar instances because the restoration was from eighty-five to almost one hundred percent perfect. In only a few instances, perhaps less than one percent, was the print not restorable.

Later when seeing the restored work on the wall of the Lester Arwin temporary gallery, it was difficult to believe the success of the venture. It is with some pride that I viewed the restored work of so many wonderful artists. I was glad that I had been able to help such a distinguished gallery director.

REGISTRATION AND TRANSFER FOR COLOR WORK

In color lithography it is necessary to register and transfer the work from one stone to another. There are three methods by which this can be accomplished. Regardless of the method employed, first select the color that is most complete or total in the overall characteristic of the composition. For example, in some compositions this may be the stone that has the black and white painting. Under many circumstances and perhaps most of the time, the stone that has the most overall coverage of the composition is the stone that carries the gray color. In any event select the stone on which appears the greatest amount of work from an all-over standpoint. This stone should give a key reference for all of the other colors and black. The key stone should be painted and/or drawn first. When it is completed, proceed with the method chosen.

The first and simplest, but not the best, is to trace the work accurately in detail on tracing paper. At each end, outside the work, approximately one inch in the margin, place a pinpoint mark. These marks will establish the two points of registration. The tracing is the master design for the registration of the other stones in the composition. Prepare a piece of sanguine or dragon's blood transfer paper. Dragon's blood is a red chalk that is completely inert and free from grease. It is desirable, from the standpoint of economy, after preparing this type of tracing paper to keep it for future use. Take a fresh sheet of tracing paper and pour onto it a small amount of red chalk or dragon's blood. Using the fingers or a cloth, rub the powder thoroughly into the tracing paper until the pores of the paper are completely filled. Put the excess dust back in the container. This prepared paper will last for years if it is carefully stored. Line up the margins around the work on the stone. Put the tracing on the stone for the correct reading and fasten with Scotch tape. Slide the chalk-prepared paper under the tracing and proceed with the tracing. With work that does not require completely accurate registration, this method is reasonably adequate. In marking the points of registration at each end of the work, be sure that they do not enlarge from stone to stone. It has been found that a dry point needle is a good tool with which to make the registration points.

The second and most used method is the transfer from stone to stone through printing. Grind the stones for the edition and have them at your disposal. Place the master stone, that has been drawn and prepared, on the press and set the press up for printing. On a hard paper similar to either bond or a clay offset paper, pull a proof in black for each stone to be transferred. Number these proofs as they are pulled so that one is able to transfer them in the same order. Gum the master stone and store it in the rack. Place a freshly grained stone on the press, and set it up for printing. Dampen the surface with a little turpentine on a clean cloth; fan until mat dry. Cut out the corners and registration points of one of the proofs, as described under Paper Transfer. Place the proof carefully without making more than one contact on the face of the turpentine-dampened stone, and run through the press (Fig. 39). Remove backing and check to see that the registration marks are clearly indicated. Proceed in the same manner with the remaining stones in the particular composition. As soon as they are completed, dampen the face of each stone with water and wash out as much of the transferred ink as possible with a clean cloth and turpentine. Follow the order of transferring. Wipe clean and allow only the lightest visible image to remain. Drill in the registration points with a sharp scraper or a thin-bladed knife and cover with a clean sheet of newsprint paper until painted.

The third method of registration requires the making of a key stone. Under rare circumstances when highly detailed and accurate registration is required,

Figure 39. Registration for color.

a key stone is the best method. Everything that appears in each color is drawn with a pen and ink line in tusche on a separate stone. The areas are either numbered, or cross-hatched at the edges of separation to show various differences of color so they can be easily read. The procedure for transfer is the same as under the second method. The key stone has no other use than for transferring, and it is never printed in the edition.

INK ROLLING

The technique and characteristics of ink rolling should be studied and practiced with close attention. There are leather hand grips for the handles of the roller which are a great asset during the long work of printing the edition. If the leather ink holders fit the hand and the roller well, one still has a great amount of control over the roller. They eliminate blisters but also curtail the control and sensitivity of handling the roller. If I use them, it is generally after all the preliminary problems have been solved.

The proper method of holding the ink roller is not as one would normally take hold of any other round handle. In the case of the ink roller the thumb should be a free agent on top and not circled underneath the handle (Fig. 26). This helps to prevent blisters and also allows for much greater flexibility of the roller in the fingers and the palm of the hand. Occasionally in some colorwork it is necessary to put the thumb underneath to lift off some of the weight of the roller (Fig. 38). This seldom is needed and is used only in light or flat colorwork in order to avoid overrolling or roller lap marks. Otherwise the normal procedure is to take the roller in the cup of the hand with the fingers circling it and the thumb on top. It is recommended that one learn to roll without leather grips in order to develop rolling technique. It will at first have a tendency to produce blisters, but more importantly, it will allow the person to become sensitive to the pressure and the overall control of the roller. As soon as one has solved the problems of ink rolling, the leather grips are recommended. Using leather grips to begin with is not recommended because it would take too long to learn proper rolling. It may be interesting to mention that this summer a three-year commission was completed for Heritage Workshop. During the printing of 30 editions, totaling 1500 prints, no leather grips were used at any time, and at no time was there the slightest indication of a blister.

From a basic standpoint the stone is dampened to repel ink where there is no work. The dampness is also to some extent on the composition, and this dampness obviously must be picked up by the roller before the work can be inked. From that fact we have the constant relationship between moisture and grease. In order to charge the roller the moisture must be worked out on the ink slab. In order to ink the stone, the roller must be passed over the stone a sufficient number of times to put ink onto the stone in the desired amount. This requires about four to eight passes of the roller on the ink slab to charge the roller, and about the same number of rolls on the stone to deposit the ink on the work. The number of rolls varies, of course, with the work and the size of the stone. At the end of each pass, twist the wrist and move the fingers forward so that when the roller comes down it is in a new position and is not just being charged in the same location. About every four or five passes the ink roller should be turned end-for-end to level out the ink on the ink slab and on the roller (Fig. 27). After the ink roller has been charged, the ink is rolled on the stone. It is again important to twist the roller each time during the inking so that it is constantly being changed to a fresh position. However, when inking the work, the ink roller is not turned end-for-end.

One should learn to control the positions of the arms so that the roller starts and stops in a definite location, forward and back, without going over the edge of the stone. This prevents depositing ink on the margins of the stone. There should be a crescendo-diminuendo type of pressure used, so that at the end of the stroke the roller does not stop dead on either the work or the edge, but is in constant movement off, either forward or back. One roll of the stone is considered one back-and-forth cycle. One inking of the stone is considered to be four to eight rolls. The fastness of the roll has to do with the sharpness of the deposit. In other words, if the rolling is rapid, the ink is building up sharply and not very much ink is deposited; whereas the slower and harder the roll, the more ink is being deposited. The forward movement in rolling deposits ink and the backward part of the cycle lifts the ink up. In spot rolling, one is constantly putting more pressure on and gradually lifting the pressure off to prevent sharp edges as much as possible. It takes a little time to feel completely relaxed in using the ink roller. The best suggestion that can be offered is that it is better at the beginning to learn to control the various aspects in a relaxed attitude, rather than to consider the work precious and tighten up.

DRYING TIME FOR ROLLING

During the hot summer months it will be noticed that the work drys very rapidly, not allowing sufficient time for inking or printing. In round numbers, one has approximately six or seven seconds of rolling time before there is too little moisture on the stone to proceed. The normal remedy to consider would be to put more moisture on the stone; however, this completely defeats the purpose, because excess moisture on the stone will merely be picked up by the ink roller, which in turn will become saturated with moisture; the moisture will then become interspersed with the ink, and the ink will not stick at all. Keep in mind that the moisture must remain constant, regardless of the time of year. If on a hot day it is found that the ink rolling time has been cut down to two or three seconds which is insufficient to roll the stone up to full force, one of two things is suggested. The one generally used is to dissolve a few grains of coarse salt in the wiping water. This will slow up the drying time without ill effects on the work. Consequently it will give one approximately the same time that one normally has in the colder months. The other possibility is to add two tablespoons of stale beer to the wiping solution. This also will prevent too rapid drying during summer months.

DOUBLE BLACK PRINTING

The aesthetic quality of some compositions is increased by developing a double black. This can be achieved in several ways. The most obvious is to have two black stones with two different prepared black inks. A variation on the above is to paint and/or draw the composition and prepare the work as if to print. Instead of printing at this phase, place the stone on the sink and grind the work out to various degrees. The grinding may be to any degree, even in part to eliminate some areas. If reprepared at this phase and printed, the overall appearance would have a gray and soft gritty effect. However, the purpose in this instance was to establish a ghost image of grays, over which a more positive image could be painted or drawn. Consequently the next step after the partial grinding is to counteretch the entire surface and thereby resensitize it for further work. At this stage paint or draw the more positive aspects of the composition. Prepare the stone as if it were a new work, and follow the standard procedure for printing. Through this procedure a double black will be established that has a figure and ground relationship.

The third possibility is easier and is used quite extensively in colorwork. The darkest color in the composition is painted underneath and registered to the black in selected areas. As a result where the black is not reinforced by the secondary dark color, it will appear flatter than in the other areas. The reinforced black areas will appear as a slightly glossier and denser black.

COUNTERETCH

The counteretch is used when corrections are needed that require the addition of new crayon or tusche within areas that are either unworked or where it is desired to add more to the composition. There are two materials used for counteretch: about a 40 percent solution of acetic acid, or a saturated solution of alum. Either will be completely effective. Wash the work thoroughly and remove all traces of gum from the entire stone. It is highly recommended to have a sponge that is kept separate from all the other sponges and used only for counteretching. This is the only way to be sure that the sponge is completely devoid of gum. After the work has been thoroughly washed, fan dry. Dampen the surface of the stone with the special sponge. Flood the areas to be counteretched with a sponge saturated with either of the counteretch materials named. Let the solution remain for a period of approximately two minutes, and rinse off thoroughly with water. Wipe clean with the special sponge and fan dry. Allow the stone to remain open during the time in which the new additions are made. As soon as the additions are completed, prepare the stone, following normal procedure as if the area where work has been added were a new stone. Merely regum the part where work has not been added. Finish the procedure by smoothing down to a thin layer of gum and let rest for six hours.

One further comment on counteretch is to indicate that the purpose of counteretching is to negate all the prior preparation, as far as the chemistry of the work on the stone is concerned. In doing this there is a slight corrosive action that has a tendency to coarsen the previous work; therefore, counteretch should be avoided unless it is essential.

ACID WASH FOR PREPARATION

We have discussed in detail the various possibilities for the preparation of work. A method that is not often used is the acid gum wash. It is not essential and does not improve or add to the other methods that have been described except perhaps on rare occasions. After employing the method successfully on numerous prints, it still cannot be stated with assurance that the method has a clear advantage. At one time it may have held greater importance; however, not knowing of this method in my early investigations, the other techniques were extended and improved to the degree that there seemed little need for any other technique.

The acid gum wash method of preparation is used when there is a large quantity of fine light detail, either intermixed or adjacent to heavy solid blacks in the composition. Dust the work with French chalk and powdered resin. Place the stone to be prepared at approximately a 30 degree angle on the grinding sink. For a medium large stone prepare a gallon of solution composed of ½ cup gum arabic, 2 teaspoons of nitric acid, and water. The amount may be proportionate to the size of the stone. This formula will be a weak solution. It will be enough to wash down the entire face of the stone several times. Pour the solution from the top edge, covering the entire face of the stone and let it drain in the sink. Continue with this process, hesitating slightly between each washing until the entire gallon of solution has been used. When completed, rinse with water and let the work drain. Place the stone in a flat position, fan dry, and cover with a thin coat of pure gum arabic. One would think that under this procedure, the great amount of water would dissolve the work. Instead the constant bathing of the mild solution prepares the stone and work for the next phase. Allow the stone to rest for six hours and follow standard procedure. The use of any method is a matter of judgment, and the application should have serious consideration. Technique at most is only a means to art quality, and it is not important how the result is obtained.

BROKEN STONE

Stone transfer may be necessary because of grease mounting causing a damaged and noncontrollable stone, and occasionally it is required because of a broken stone. Ink the work as clearly as possible under the circumstances and close it with a pure solution of gum arabic. In case the work is being transferred because of a broken stone, it is necessary to procure a piece of lightweight band iron. The band iron should be two inches wide and formed in two sections (Fig. 40). The sections should be based on the length and width of the stone as to shape and size of the outside dimension. Bend the band iron so that it does not meet at top or bottom by one inch and at these points bend a one-inch right-angle extension. Drill two holes three-sixteenths of an inch in diameter, equally spaced in each extension. Place the band iron around the edge of the stone and fasten together with one-eighth-inch by two-inch bolts. Slowly and evenly bring the band into tension, top and bottom, until the broken stone is held solidly together. Under most circumstances the supported stone will be strong enough to allow for a transfer. Use gummed paper for the transfer. The procedure from this point will be the same for either uncontrollable grease or a broken stone and will require the information on gum paper, transfer, and transfer ink.

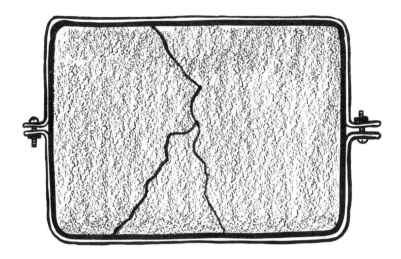

Figure 40.   Preparation of broken stone.

PAPER TRANSFER

Under the heading of paper transfer there are essentially two categories of paper to be considered. One is a gum-prepared paper. This may be purchased commercially and is, in my opinion, the best. If this paper is not available, a piece of soft thin paper may be gummed. If you prepare your own gummed paper, the method that I have found to work easiest is to put a thin coat of gum on a large stone. Smooth this down in a polydirectional manner with your hand. Take a piece of soft thin paper of the size needed, spread this on the face of the wet gum, lift it up, spread it a second time, and then remove it. Pin or tape it down and allow to dry. It is important that the gum is thin enough in mixture with water so that only a light coat of gum is transferred to the surface of the paper. Although slightly more crude than a commercial gummed paper, a paper so prepared will work in an adequate manner. Any direct work may be done on gummed paper. This eliminates involved techniques that require removal and addition; however, there is still a wide range of possibilities. Do not at any time use water tusche or any combination that includes water. When tusche is required, use a turpentine- or benzine-tusche mixture. This will not disturb or melt the gum because of the separation of binders.

The second type of paper transfer does not require a gum-surfaced paper. Generally speaking, any paper can be used for ungummed lithographic transfers. Some papers work better than others; for example, a thick paper is generally too insensitive, whereas a very soft paper, although it will allow for transfer, absorbs some of the grease into the body of the paper, and hence the work cannot be completely transferred. A little experimentation on types of paper transfer is recommended. Feel perfectly free to use a fairly thin hard paper, the thickness of a mediumweight bond. Again the work should be done with crayon or with thick turpentine tusche, never water tusche. It is well to keep

190

in mind that if one desires the work to be read from one direction, it will be necessary to consider this at the start.

Either of these methods is interesting to pursue when one is away from the studio on a trip, and heavy equipment is not available. When ready to transfer the paper drawing or painting onto a stone, it is recommended that the stone be ground with either a 2F or 3F grain. The reason for this is to keep the fine grain of the paper consistent with the stone.

Both the gummed paper and plain paper are transferred by the following procedure. Put the freshly prepared stone on the bed of the press and set the press up as for printing. Cut out the corners of the paper to be transferred, as shown in Fig. 41. Dampen the stone with water several times, so that the moisture is allowed to go as deeply as possible into the stone. Fan dry and dampen again. This creates greater absorption and a cooler and more deeply moist stone. Re-dampen the stone and fan until the surface of the stone becomes mat damp but not wet.

Carefully place the paper to be transferred onto the stone, cover with one sheet of damp backing and two sheets of dry backing, plus the pressboard. Run through the press four continuous back-and-forth cycles. Remove the pressboard, so as not to disturb the transfer paper, and then remove the two dry sheets of backing. Thoroughly dampen the remaining backing sheet with water on a sponge. Run through the press four more cycles. Again remove the backing, including the dampened sheet this time, and thoroughly dampen the paper used for transfer, but avoid excess water which could cause a smudge. Cover with fresh dry backing and the pressboard, and run four more complete cycles through the press. Remove the backing and carefully peel or roll back the transfer paper, as close to a horizontal pull as possible. If it is noticed when the back is lifted a slight way that all of the transfer has not taken place, dampen

Figure 41. Preparation for transfer.

and repeat the operation for four more cycles. If, on the other hand, most of the transfer has been made, continue to peel off the transfer paper and fan the work dry. Dust with French chalk and cover with a coat of pure gum arabic. Let the stone rest for two or three hours. After the rest period gently dampen off the gum with a sponge and water. Take a lean roller and ink the work slightly so that it gains a small amount. Do not try to bring it up much darker than the transfer image. Fan dry, dust with chalk, and give the work a mild etch with a mixture of acid and gum that shows a very slight effervescence when tested on the side of the stone. Smooth the gum mixture and fan dry. Let rest again for six hours and follow a standard wash-out and roll-up procedure.

When using the gum-prepared paper, the procedure is the same with but one exception. The press cycle should be completed while there is still an amount of moisture remaining in the transfer paper. If it is rolled dry, the gum preparation will make it completely adhere to the stone, and it will not be possible to remove it except by rubbing the paper gradually out. This is not recommended, simply because it is not necessary and could damage the work. Under a moist condition the paper will peel off in the same manner as previously described. An interesting observation here is that with the gummed paper it is not possible to add more work to the stone after the transfer, except through the standard procedure of resensitizing. However, with the unprepared paper, prior to gumming, more artwork can be added and the whole work gummed and etched at one time.

WHEN THE WORK WILL NOT ROLL UP

There are times when a work has been prepared in a normal fashion, but because of extremely cold weather or because the work was drawn too lightly or with too hard a crayon, it simply will not roll up. One can see the ghost image when the stone is damp, but, in spite of continuous rolling, the ink will not deposit. The first suggestion is to fatten the ink more than normal by adding linseed oil and attempt full, slow rolling to bring the work up to a full charging of ink. If the work does not respond to this treatment, eliminate further attempts to soften the ink. Most of the time lean work appears on fringe areas where the preparation needed for the darks has been slightly strong for the delicate areas, or the delicate areas were perhaps too delicate in the first place. When the light areas are too lean to respond to a slightly fatter ink, it becomes necessary to use a special technique. It is advisable to proceed in the order given, rather than employ the most radical method at the start.

At the conclusion of the wash-out stage, instead of rolling up the work in ink, dampen the stone with the sponge, take a clean cloth into which has been rubbed some printing ink, and lightly rub the light fringe areas to bring them up to a stronger image. The moisture must be constant. The rubbing action creates a small amount of friction that has a warming effect. This makes the grease in the stone a little more active, and as a result it will take additional ink. Sometimes blowing breath on the area will help greatly in warming the grease content and will make it more active. After the grays have been rubbed up, proceed with the normal rolling of the entire stone. There are occasions when very heavy work is adjacent and interrelated in position to light grays. It is desirable under such circumstances to rub up the entire stone, paying more attention to the specialized areas than to the general areas. This in itself helps to prevent the overrolling of grays. It is understandable that the amount of ink that it necessary to produce a solid black would be excessive for delicate areas under extended rolling.

The rub-up procedure eliminates a much longer process of bringing the work up through continual proofing. Except for very lean work, proofing over fifteen or twenty prints should produce about the same result. Under this procedure there is ever present the risk of overinking the areas that take ink normally. Almost without exception one learns intuitively to spot roll. However, the standard rolling practice is more characteristic of the second and third charging of the work rather than the first. The first rolling, in every instance that I can think of, is special to the work. Consequently when one is learning to roll a particular work through the wash-out and rollup periods, the work on the stone itself indicates the best manner and procedure for the eventual printing of the edition. Once this is learned it is only slightly varied throughout the entire edition. The manner of rolling is fitted to the work itself. Consequently, a heavier section in the composition will require shorter rolls, and the lighter sections in the composition will require either fewer or lighter rolls. It is important that the habit of spot rolling be consistently employed in order to keep an even edition of prints and to prevent the need for additional washouts or special treatments.

After the rub-up has been attempted without sufficient success, the third possibility should be tried. Under this circumstance, wash the stone out normally, dampen the stone, pour onto the dampened stone about one teaspoonful of liquid asphaltum, and rub the asphaltum into the entire stone, keeping the stone damp throughout the process. It will be noticed that the asphaltum, like the ink, will stick to the work. Where the work needs to be brought up to a fatter degree, rub more vigorously. Wipe off the excess with a cloth, keep the stone moist, and proceed with the rolling. Sometimes it is necessary to use a combination of asphaltum rub-up in conjunction with an ink rub-up. In all situations one should judge the work and the problem and select the least severe kind of treatment to solve the problem before proceeding to more radical types of corrective measures. The two types of wash-out described earlier are usable for these special techniques. It is preferable, when possible, however, to employ the dry-gummed method of wash-out because it allows an extended period of time for work. The method used will depend on the condition of the work.

In the event that the stone still will not allow a proper roll-up after using the preceding techniques, the last possibility may be tried. This process is more precarious but sometimes succeeds when everything else fails. Take two strips of cardboard about one inch wide and place them on the margins of the stone. Take a narrow strip of white pine saturated in alcohol and place it on top of the two pieces of cardboard. The cardboard will prevent the saturated wood from touching the face of the stone. The extreme evaporation will have the effect of activating the grease and bringing it up to the surface. Follow this by taking a small heating fan, such as a hair drier, and exposing the face of the work to warm air for two or three minutes. Dampen the stone and immediately roll. When as much ink has been deposited as possible, fan dry and follow with a wash-out, roll-up procedure using asphaltum. Wipe clean, fan dry, dampen, and roll up to full force. This last procedure may endanger the work and should only be employed when all else has failed and there is nothing to lose.

WHEN THE WORK DARKENS

There are four main methods of establishing control when after a few proofs or prints it is noticed that the work is beginning to darken.

1. Immediately pull an uninked newspaper print to remove excessive ink. Follow with a sharp single roll, and examine the work on the stone. Keep the stone damp during this time. If on examination the darkening does not seem excessive, the procedure is to undercharge the roller by scraping the ink slab down and rolling off as much ink as possible. Use fast, sharp rolling with the undercharged ink roller. Bring the work up to just under full force. Fan dry and cover with a thin coat of gum to which has been added 3 drops of nitric acid to $\frac{1}{2}$ cup of gum arabic. This amount of acid will have no noticeable effect, but it will act as a very mild cleaning and degreasing agent. Fan the work dry. Open the stone and pull newspaper proofs to determine whether the work is back to where it should be held. If the work will stand regular rolling and not take excessive ink, the printing may be continued.

2. In extreme situations where one has neglected for several prints to observe a mounting situation, considerable damage may have been done. This would require a more drastic treatment to restore the work to its original form. In such a case, wash out the stone so that it is completely clean, and fan dry. Dampen the stone and roll up the work to approximately half strength for the grays. Disregard the darks. Take a solution of $\frac{1}{2}$ cup of gum and 5 drops of nitric acid, and apply with a small brush to the areas or spots that have gained or filled. The length of time that the brushed-on gum should remain

in contact with the questioned area should not exceed a total of one or two seconds. This may not solve the problem, but it will noticeably degrease the offending areas. Scrape the roller down, and mix a very stiff nonfat ink. Charge the roller slightly and fast roll the work, primarily for the gray areas. When these areas are up to their original form, rub up the darks separately with a cloth and a little of the ink that is on the slab. If one is fortunate, the offending areas will now be under control.

3. If they are not, fan the stone dry and dust with French chalk. Take a needle, such as a dry-point needle, and prick into the offending areas with a vertical stroke until the work has been reopened and the grease has been removed to the approximate degree that had been established in the original drawing. Any areas so worked should be immediately treated with a mild gum acid. This is removed with the end of the sponge to which has been added a solution of gum arabic, consisting of ½ cup of fresh gum and 5 drops of nitric acid. When all of this procedure has been completed, regum the stone. Allow a fairly thick coat to remain on the face of the work, cover with a fresh sheet of newsprint paper, and allow to rest a few hours. This entire procedure may need to be done more than once. It is believed, however, that if the procedure does not accomplish the desired effect after being worked in this corrective manner twice, it may be considered that the damage is permanent, and any further work will require a compromise with the intended results. In extreme cases where it is not desirable to accept a compromise the work should be transferred to a fresh stone.

4. Take a freshly-grained stone, ground with either 2F or 3F carborundum or its equivalent. It is necessary to use a finely grained stone, regardless of the type of grain of the stone from which the work is being transferred. The reason for this is that if a coarser grained surface is used, some of the detail of the work would be lost in the valleys, since it would be impossible to register the mountains and valleys of the grain of the old stone on the new stone. Wash out the work to be transferred and roll it up as sharp as possible, using a special transfer ink. It will be found that this ink feels gritty and coarser than standard printing ink. Work it well with the ink knife to soften. If necessary for proper rolling, add a few drops of linseed oil. After the work is rolled in transfer ink, fan the stone dry. Pull a sharp, full proof on gum-prepared transfer paper. As a safety precaution in case the first attempt is not successful, it is wise to gum the damaged stone and put it in temporary storage. Place the newly ground stone on the press and set up as for printing. Dampen the stone with water, fan dry, redampen the stone, and fan until mat, but not dry, then quickly place the transfer proof on the stone. Place a dampened piece of backing paper over the transfer proof and then normal backing and pressboard. Run the assembly through the press according to the directions outlined in the section on paper transfer.

Emil Weddige
"Repose"
edition 12
30" x 22½" (horizontal)

15

LITHOGRAPHY IN COLOR

ANY print in color must be arrived at through the medium, and not be colored later or retouched in any manner. Hence, the proper reference in lithography is to state that the work is a lithograph in color or a color lithograph. It is never correctly referred to as a colored lithograph because this connotes that the work has been colored other than through the medium. There are occasionally fakes or false color adaptations; however, they are easily detected and are not acceptable as within the medium by any print authority.

Preliminary to starting work in color, it is essential that a decision be made on the approach to the interpretation of the idea or concept of the artwork. It is recommended that a general understanding of the color involved be reached in small sketch form. A log should be kept of procedure, and a periodic evaluation should be made of any changes of attitude that take place as the work progresses. With regard to other considerations, the artist is free to move in any direction he chooses as the work develops. It is generally accepted that lithography in color means two or more stones, one of which is color. This is a generously broad interpretation. In the minimum interpretation when only two stones are involved, it is obvious that one stone has the color and is used as an appendage to the structure.

As lithography in color develops to more complex interpretations and involves more colors and consequently more stones, the emphasis shifts from color in a supporting role to a combination of colors forming the structure itself. The number and relationship of warm and cool colors determine the number of separate stones. For example, in a composition involving three basic colors, not counting combinations, one stone is considered a master stone which is primarily the structure of the idea of the composition. Another stone presents the image of the color concept and the third stone is the interlocking stone or the one that has the function of tying the other stones together compositionally. It is possible to make a very involved color lithograph on one stone. This is not unique; one need only follow and apply the directions related to area graining and resensitization. The one-stone method has the weak advantage of saving time, but it also has critical disadvantages, the most important of which is that the progress of the work becomes inflexible and rigid, and the work loses grays. In spite of the disadvantages, if I owned but one stone, it would be easy to subscribe to the method. For our purpose, we will consider separate stones for each color.

When the idea of the composition and the number of colors involved have been determined, the work is ready to proceed. It is advisable at this time to check the free stones in the supply and make a selection of whatever number is required. It is preferable that these stones be grained and prepared for use; however, except for the first stone, the others can wait and be prepared after the completion of the painting or drawing of the first stone. This first stone may be any one of those involved in the composition, but generally it is either the interlocking color or the black. When the first stone has been completed, it should be prepared in the normal manner, through first preparation, washout and roll-up, and then be allowed to rest for at least 24 hours. You are referred to Chapter 11 on these two items. During the resting time of the stones, there are a few things that can be checked and prepared. Let us assume that the number of stones involved have been grained and are ready for use. It is always a wise procedure at this time to clean the studio and check supplies. It is surprising how many times a person overlooks a minor detail in preparation that can become major in consequence. Read again the section on special techniques and have a firm understanding of stone transfer for color registration, as well as the comments on paper registration and pin registration.

We should be ready now for transfer, if the stone transfer is used. Place the stone that has been prepared on the bed of the press and set the press up for printing. Wash the stone out, roll it up, and pull newsprint proofs to determine that the stone is up to full printing force. Ink the stone and pull a clean print on a glazed or hard surface paper similar to bond for each stone that is to be registered. Mark these in numerical order as they are taken, so that the drying time of the ink can be controlled when they are transferred to the freshly ground stones. When you have pulled sufficient proofs, roll the master stone up sharp, fan dry, and close with a thin coat of gum. Remove this stone from the bed of the press and put it in the storage rack. Take one of the freshly grained stones and set up the press as if making ready to print. Take the first transfer pulled and cut each corner out square to the margin of the work and also cut a V notch to within approximately 1/16 of an inch of the registration points (Fig. 41). This will allow for the centering of the print on the stone and also for checking to see that the registration points are within the surface of the stone. Set this prepared transfer print aside, and if you have an assistant, let him or her prepare the other transfer papers, being cautious not to touch the face of the paper in which the composition is involved. Take a clean cloth and dampen the stone with turpentine so that it is wet all over but not flooded. Wipe horizontally and vertically so that there is an even deposit of dampness over the face of the stone. Hand fan until it loses the wet shininess and becomes mat. At this instant take the first prepared transfer print, being careful not to touch the stone until the correct position is located, then gently lower the transfer into place. Put on normal backing and run through the press one way as in regular printing. Remove the backing carefully, so as not to slur or jar the transfer paper. Before removing the transfer proof, check at both ends to see that the registration points have been transferred. If they are not clear, rub them with your finger. When this is done, remove the transfer proof, and it will be found that the image of the first stone has been transferred to the fresh stone. Follow this procedure throughout with the number of stones that are involved in the particular composition. If the work has proceeded at a consistent pace, the length of time for the total operation will vary between 15 and approximately 25 minutes. This is sufficient to fix a stain on each of the new stones. It is not recommended that a very much longer time elapse.

Starting with the first stone transferred and working in this order, dampen the stone with water as in a wash-out. Take a clean cloth dampened with turpentine and remove all of the transferred ink that can be washed off without scrubbing and still leave a stained image on the stone. Throughout this procedure constantly change the wiping cloth to a clean location. When completed, wash with clean water and fan dry. Proceed with the other stones in the edition. As soon as the stones are dry, take a scraper and lightly drill a pinpoint hole in the center of each registration point. These registration holes should not be large in diameter and should be drilled with as little pressure as is possible so that the edges are not chipped. Prior to painting or drawing, the stones should be covered with clean newsprint paper that is taped down and marked if there is a difference in grain. This will protect them from dust and grease until they are ready for use. If space permits, I like to arrange all of the stones in the work area and paint on them from one to the other. This allows freedom of interpretation and a spontaneity of movement. Under ordinary circumstances the painting follows the related importance of the colors and not the relationship of printing. However, this is not essential so, depending on your inclination, the subsequent stones should be painted. When each is completed, prepare it for printing, using the standard methods of procedure.

In color lithography, it is generally desirable to print from the light to the dark colors. There are two standard approaches to printing the edition. On a relatively simple composition or one that is clear in interpretation, proceed as in black and white, or in other words, determine that each printing is a final decision. In more complex compositions where the final assembly of stones is obscure, it is sometimes advisable to pull what is called an essay. An essay is a trial run of each stone, printing a light, dark, warm or cool interpretation of each color so as to have a comparison of the various combinations. In this manner one is able to check the final results and make any changes or corrections before the printing of the final edition. When the essay procedure is followed, considerably more time and work are involved, and this procedure is only recommended when there is a definite need for it. On commissions where a specific end product must be presented before the editions are completed, it is essential that an essay be pulled.

Most times I prefer and follow the practice of proofing in and making a final decision on each color in its separate form. It will be assumed that the latter will be followed for this present discussion. In keeping with this, select the stone that is to be printed first. Set it up on the press. If this stone is not the one that was used for registration, counteretch the two registration points, touch each with a pinpoint spot of tusche, and follow with a gum etch. It is not necessary to wait for a resting time for these retouched points. They will be transferred on the paper in the color that is being printed and will be the points of registration for the other stones. Pull several newsprint proofs until the work is up to full force before starting the printing on good paper.

The paper for the edition should be arranged so that the watermark will be right side up and in a convenient location to the press. Pull the first proof on good paper. Generally the first proof will be light and some adjustment may be necessary in either the consistency of the ink or the pressure of the press. Keep in mind that, unlike black and white, the printing is generally on dry paper. The reason for this is that wet paper is stretched going through the press and this stretching sometimes amounts to three-eighths of an inch which would be disastrous where registration is called for (see Chapter 14). The pressure as a result will need to be slightly heavier for color printing and the ink adjusted slightly softer than has been your usual experience. At this time set up two pieces of wood and position two nails in each for the centering of the composition on the paper (Figs. 42 and 43). This may take a little adjustment until the work is located properly. These slabs of wood are put adjacent to the stone each time that inking has been completed and removed after the paper has been placed on the stone. After a full-force clean print has been pulled, examine it

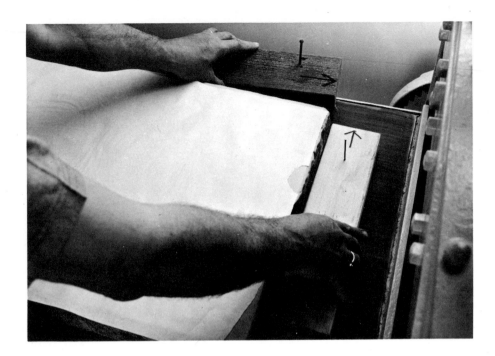

Figure 42. Placing guides.

critically in every aspect to determine that the value is correct, that the over-lays correspond to your thinking, and most importantly that the white areas have been guarded for their eventual luminosity. When a firm decision has been reached, proceed with the printing of the edition.

Check each time to see that the registration points have been printed. The scraper sometimes has a tendency not to reach these registration points in full force, and rubbing with a smooth piece of wood or your fingernail will bring this up. As the prints are pulled, place them carefully on the work table with a clean piece of newsprint paper over the face between each print. Do not move or handle the prints once they have been placed in the stack. One of the first prints pulled should be set aside and used as a model for the printing of the edition. If there is any reason to doubt the quality or to question the gaining of any area, it is advisable to stop work and make the necessary corrections. You are referred to the chapter on Methods and Special Techniques for these corrections or adjustments.

When the printing of the first color of the edition has been completed, allow the prints to dry overnight before handling. Dust them the next day with French chalk, applying it with a piece of cotton and covering the entire face of the inked area. Wipe the work so that no loose residue of chalk remains on the surface of the print. As this is being done, examine the prints for full force, as well as cleanness. Should there be any thumbmarks caused by handling the paper, you are strongly advised to guard against repeating this in any future printing. Your hands must be clean in handling the paper; otherwise, by the time one has printed five or six stones there is apt to be a very badly damaged edition. Soiled prints can be avoided by keeping the ink slab, the handles of the roller, and the ink knife in immaculate condition.

The edition should be edited after the printing of each color for evenness and quality. It will be found that one or two prints are either faultily rolled or are light. Separate uneven prints, so that they will be the first prints to be used for proofs on the next stone. After the edition has been carefully examined, take a push-pin or needle and prick a small hole, the smaller the better, in the center of each of the registration points that have been printed.

Figure 43.   Register paper.

This is a good time to discuss registration points. Practically any type of pin or needle may be used; however, the kind that is preferred is one that has been made from the handles of small old watercolor brushes. Cut off about two inches of the end of the brush handle. Into the cut end is pressed a sewing needle from which the head or eye has been removed. This makes a very lightweight, well-balanced pin and it can be used easily between the two fingers and the thumb for placing the paper into registration holes. (Note Fig. 44.)

Each stone in the composition should be printed following the procedure outlined for the first stone. The work is dusted after each printing with the exception of the last color on which the dusting is omitted. It is recommended that the work be organized so that there is a day of drying between each color. In some seasons of the year or because of a number of overprintings, the work may take slightly longer to dry. When the printing of the last stone is completed, a canceled proof may be pulled. When this is desired, roll the stone up to printing strength and with a razor blade scrape an X or some large mark through the face of the work. It is convenient to merely take a cloth with a little turpentine and wash out a path through the face of the composition. A proof of the cancellation is pulled on good paper for the record. After two or three days of drying, the edition should receive the final editing and cataloguing.

Figure 44.   Color registration.

Artists have different viewpoints on the size of the editions. Generally, I prefer an edition of 25 to 50 prints, depending on the desire of the moment or the amount of paper on hand. This question, of course, is generally settled before the work is started. Let us assume that we wish to have an edition of 25 prints, and there are four colors involved in the composition. In this instance it is recommended that 29 prints be pulled, one extra for each color. This allows latitude for error. The final editing will determine the exact size of the edition. Examine the entire group of prints carefully, and any print that does not meet the quality of the print used as a model, or what the French refer to as the *bon tirage*, set aside and exclude from the edition. If one is fortunate, there will be, under the example chosen, 25 first-class prints. No print should remain as part of the edition unless it is of the best quality. In the most accepted practice, these should be signed on the right at the bottom, and the edition number should be placed on the left at the bottom, along with the title if there is one.

Titles are curious things, and a printmaker soon begins to doubt the need when so much writing is required. However, one experience of not writing the titles on my work cured me for all time. One fall a large group of prints were sent out to several dealers, and answering letters and telephone calls became a headache because of the difficulty of trying to determine which print we were discussing from descriptions without titles. I subscribe now to the practice of writing titles on prints without comment and firmly recommend it to anyone else.

The edition numbering may be done in one of two ways, either (ed. 25) or (1/25, 2/25), etc. In this example if the four remaining prints that have been set aside from the edition are also of first quality, one could make the edition 29 and number them correspondingly. However, I prefer to hold my editions to a definite round number and always reserve two or three prints to be designated as artist's proofs, which can become presentation prints, or artist's trial proofs if there is a slight discrepancy in the workmanship. If I have used either a printer or an assistant, a print will be so designated. Many collectors prefer one of the latter classifications. If any one of the prints falls short of high quality, my policy is to destroy it without delay.

Some systematic log should be kept on all work so that on any given work the type and number of prints signed are recorded along with any special characteristics of the work. Tamarind Workshop has established an excellent method for recording prints. It follows very closely the procedure as outlined; however, in their case they go even further and document the entire procedure through a curator. When the editing has been completed, it is usual to put a piece of jeweler's tissue paper between each print and store them in numerical order in the print file, pending their future homes.

Emil Weddige
"Carabela Columbus"
edition 45
20½″ x 26¼″ (vertical)

Emil Weddige

16

COLLECTOR AND ARTIST

IT has long been my contention that, although artists may differ in many ways, in one respect they arrive at the same conclusion. Work needs to be seen to be purchased, and the question of what to do with work when it is completed eventually takes on major proportions. Especially if one is to devote a lifetime to producing it. There is only so much space in which to store work, and obviously it would be rather dismal to endlessly acquire stacks of drawers or to be constructing buildings for storage. The example of a sculptor whose sole purpose is to make monumental bronzes that reach twenty feet into the air and weigh ten tons each clinches any discussion and dispels all doubt about the misconception of the artist and the ivory tower.

The artist is an inseparable part of society. This relationship to remain healthy must be based on mutual respect and confidence. Museums, art galleries, and their directors are the connecting link between the public and the artist, and the role of the art critic or writer bridges communication in all directions. This overall representation should be based on carefully selected standards and on long-term association. It should be free of any questionable practice and be of unimpeachable integrity. At times fiction writers find it interesting to exaggerate some of the things that artists do or place value on, and there has been much good fun poked at artists. It is true that most artists have somewhat different points of view toward values, and at times this is not easy to understand. However, it should be admitted that food or dress at times are secondary to the intensity of other things, and artwork may or may not be less expensive than wallpaper. In spite of any isolated instance to the contrary, no one seriously questions the overall importance of art as a contributing factor in society.

Persons planning to purchase art, as well as advanced students, are constantly asking how prices on artwork are determined. Inevitably a solution to this question needs answering. First of all, one aspect should be clear. It is not believed that a person after a few efforts should rush out with the idea of a show and sales. Although somewhat far fetched, it is similar to brain surgery, self-taught. Exhibitions and sales should not be made prematurely because they can damage growth by a too early crystallization. I recall the artist, Edouard Goerg of France, commenting about the rush of young Americans to show and the general attitude in the United States where there are many introductions with quick oblivion thereafter. By contrast, in France there are distinct levels of approach to a place of importance in the world of art, and the artists and public are aware of this. Perhaps we in educational institutions and museums, art writers, and artists could make a greater effort to develop a more constructive approach to evaluation, authentication, and presentation. For the purpose here, it is assumed that, after some struggles on the artist's part, there is a need to establish a monetary value on work. There are numerous ways of setting a price on labor and talent, but in the final analysis it is up to the individual to decide which method to use, because none are very conclusive. It seems to me that the most adequate method, and the one which I follow, is to base the cost of a work on the time involved, and in the case of prints to divide that amount with the number in the edition. This reasoning suggests that the price range of prints may vary from something near fifty dollars to approximately four hundred dollars. The exceptions are in the category of high standards, involving rarity and significance. Within the realm of exception, anything, of course, may be possible.

It is good for the working contemporary artist to price work reasonably and enjoy passing to the collector the increasing value of the work. This keeps the storage drawers empty, and the artist working. The work, after all, of the contemporary artist, generally speaking, is in progress, so although it is in a limited edition, it is relatively abundant. In fact, a great asset of a print is that there is an edition, and the individual cost is the total cost divided by the number of prints in the edition. This does not mean that it has less quality; it merely means that the approximate amount of time and standard of quality involved, by comparison with a painting or sculpture of equivalent time and standard, is distributed throughout the edition. This is one of the reasons why a print is the wonderful art of the total society that it is.

One may safely say that collectors always start by hanging their walls. The questions of what is good and how one knows are unanswerable in art. It is possible to evaluate up to a point objectively, but after that, one senses the answers with insight. Consequently, such decisions are personal, and because of this aspect, it is believed that acquisitions should be based on the simple premise of taste and liking. As the individual becomes more keenly aware of qualities, the individual concept will grow with the collection. To be sure, it is possible that on this premise a few blind spots will be found. But even so, it is far more desirable to build on what is believed and felt at the time rather than to depend solely on the advice of others. This does not mean that one should not heed

Figure 45. Correct.

or even be swayed by advice. It does mean that if the collection is to be fundamentally sound and open to continuous growth, the personal aspect of the collector should be the determining factor.

There are a number of books in the reading list, and it would be advisable to systematically become informed on the subject. Your attention is particularly called to the books of Carl Zigrosser, and to the booklet of the Print Council of America entitled, *What is an Original Print?*

As the walls become hung with new works, the early attitude of matching existing colors in the rooms, and such, will be dropped. It will be found that appropriate framing will always orient the picture to its surroundings, and there is no need to be concerned with so-called clashes. This was once proven to me conclusively. A one-man show had been invited to a new and beautifully modern civic center in Midland, Michigan, designed by Alden Dow. I arrived with my work, which was all in color, and was really amazed when entering the gallery. It had two walls of white and one of black, one bright green and a fairly large entrance space-breaker wall of Venetian red. At first glance, hanging any of the print colors on the bright green seemed impossible. However, that exhibition was an excellent presentation of the work. No pieces were out

Figure 46. Correct.

of location or suffered because of the environment. In fact, the work never looked better, and the space took on its true intention and became alive to its total purpose.

As the habit and interest in acquiring new prints develop, there rapidly comes a time when it is necessary to make provision for proper storage and cataloguing. The following suggestions are recommended for all collections, even though they may be in the beginning stages. Prints should never be left unmatted for more than a few moments out of a container. The paper that the work is on is of the finest quality and should be guarded in every possible way. An accident or unintentional careless handling can easily damage the print beyond repair. In handling a print, it is best to lift it by two corners simultaneously with the print bellied in the center, or, if a one hand lift is necessary, lift the paper in a rolling motion up and in from the outside. This prevents a kink at the point of the lift. Actually a kink is a fracture of the structure of the paper and represents a most serious type of damage. It has been my experience that few people other than printmakers really know how to handle paper.

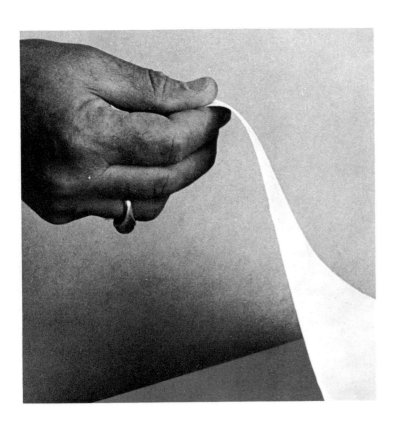

Figure 47. Incorrect.

For example, in an edition of 50 prints in five colors, each sheet will be handled a total of 20 times. The completed print should appear in every detail as a fresh sheet of paper, the same as when it was first removed from the package. It is easy to understand how disturbing it is to have the paper damaged after this professional control has been maintained. Figures 45 and 46 show the correct way to handle paper. Figures 47 and 48 show two of the incorrect ways to handle paper; each of these will damage the fiber.

Although it requires a larger mat box for storage, it is advisable to mat the print in a lightweight storage-type mat, allowing a three-inch even margin.

The opening for the work should be covered on the inside with a piece of cellophane. If this procedure has been followed, one need never hesitate to show the collection. There are a number of print boxes manufactured, and on this item one can be guided by the cost. It is desirable to select a portfolio that is strongly hinged and not over three inches deep in the storage compartment. As the collection grows and more storage boxes are added, one will become aware,

Figure 48. Incorrect.

if not before, of the need to have a careful index of each print. (This subject was discussed in Chapter 3.) Along with the information on each print, one should include all authentication papers. When purchasing a print, it is advisable to request a receipt dated and signed by the distributor, stating that the conditions of the sale are subject to and based on his representation that the described work is an original print by the artist. This procedure is a very direct and simple method of assuring your protection.

All things considered, the print collector receives unlimited return from his acquisitions. In a very modest way I have acquired over the years a small collec-

Figure 49. Examining the Parke Davis proof of "The Family."

tion that allows me to greet old friends and marvel at the new messages that are constantly being revealed. A passage from my favorite book, *Walden*, by Henry David Thoreau, is appropriate in idea—"I retained the landscape, and I have since anually carried off what it yielded without a wheelbarrow." So, also, these prints have been shared with students and friends, and with continuous seeing, the beauty of each has been multiplied and enriched.

It is my hope that this book shares with you the feeling I have for artists and the art of lithography.

BIBLIOGRAPHY

AMERICAN ART DEALERS ASSOCIATION. *Contemporary American Prints*. Introduction by Royal
   Cortissoz. New York: A. T. DeLa Mare Company, Inc., 1931. (100 plates)

BARR, ALFRED H., JR. *Matisse: His Art and His Public*. New York: The Museum of Modern
   Art, 1951.

BERRI, D. G. *The Art of Lithography*. London: The Author, 1872.

BROWN, BOLTON. *Lithography for Artists*. Chicago, Illinois: The University of Chicago Press,
   1929.

BROWNE, WARREN C. *Practical Text Book of Lithography; A Modern Treatise on the Art of
   Printing From Stone*. New York: National Lithographer, 1912.

CUMMING, DAVID. *Handbook of Lithography*. London: Adam and Charles Black, Ltd., 1919.

DEHN, ADOLF, and BARRETT, LAWRENCE. *How to Draw and Print Lithographs*. New York:
   Tudor Publishing Company, 1950.

GARDEN CITY PUBLISHING CO., INC. *Graphic Arts*. Garden City, New York: Garden City
   Publishing Co., Inc., 1929, 1930, 1932, 1933, 1936.

GRANT, ARNOLD. *Creative Lithography and How to Do It*. New York: Harper and Brothers,
   1941.

GRIFFITH, THOMAS E. *The Technique of Colour Printing by Lithography*. London: Faber and
   Faber Ltd., 1948.

HAAS, IRVIN. *A Treasury of Great Prints*. Perpetua, A. S. Barnes, 1961.

HARTRICK, ARCHIBALD S. *Lithography as a Fine Art*. London: Oxford University Press, 1932.

HULLMANDEL, CHARLES. *The Art of Drawing on Stone*. London: The Author, 1824.

IVINS, W. M., JR. *How Prints Look*. New York: Metropolitan Museum, 1943.

KISTLER, LYNTON R. *How to Make a Lithograph—A Visual Aid*. Los Angeles: The Author,
   1950. (25 plates)

LEMERCIER, ALFRED. *La Lithographie Française de 1796 à 1896 et les Arts qui s'y Rattachent*.
   Paris: Ch. Lorilleux et Cie., c 1896.

PENNELL, ELIZABETH R. *Lithography and Lithographers*. New York: The Macmillan Company, 1915.

PENNELL, JOSEPH. *The Graphic Arts* (The Scammon Lectures for 1920). Chicago, Illinois: University of Chicago Press, 1921.

THE PRINT COUNCIL OF AMERICA. *What is an Original Print?* The Print Council of America, Inc., 1961.

PETERS, HARRY T. *Currier & Ives*. Garden City, New York: Doubleday Doran & Co., Inc., 1942. (191 plates)

READ, HERBERT. *The Grass Roots of Art*. Cleveland and New York: The World Publishing Co., 1961.

RHODES, HENRY JOHN. *The Art of Lithography*. London: Scott, Greenwood & Son, 1924.

REVERDY, PIERRE. *Braque: Une Aventure Methodique*. Paris: Ed. Mourlot, 1949. (2 original Lithos. in color and 27 lithos. in black)

RICHMOND, W. D. *The Grammar of Lithography*. London: Wyman and Sons, 1886.

ROGER-MARX, CLAUDE. *French Original Engravings From Manet to the Present Time*. London-Paris-New York: The Hyperion Press, 1939. (128 plates)

SAURET, ANDRE. *Picasso Lithographe*. Notices et Catalogue Etablis Par Fernand Mourlot. 1947-1949 Editions du Livre, Monte-Carlo, 1950.

SENEFELDER, ALOIS. *The Invention of Lithography*. Translated from the original German by J. W. Muller. New York: Fuchs and Lang Manufacturing Co., 1911.

SEYMOUR, ALFRED. *Practical Lithography*. London: Scott, 1903.

WATERLOW AND SONS. *Every Man His Own Printer; or Lithography Made Easy*. London: Waterlow and Sons, 1859.

WENGENROTH, STOW. *Making a Lithograph*. New York: The Studio Publications, Inc., 1936.

ZIGROSSER, CARL. *Six Centuries of Fine Prints*. New York: Covici Friede Publishers, 1937. (488 plates)

———. *The Artist in America*. New York: Alfred A. Knopf, Inc., 1942.

LIST OF SUPPLIERS

Craftool, Inc., 396 Broadway, New York 13, New York.

Graphic Chemical and Ink Co., 714 N. Ardmore Avenue, P. O. Box #27, Villa Park, Illinois.

Grumbacker, Inc., 460 West 34th Street, New York 1, New York.

Harris Chemical Co., 5308 Blanche Avenue, Cleveland 27, Ohio.

Imperial Solution, Litho-Chemical and Supply Co. Inc., Lynbrook, New York.

Kimbers Supplies Service, 44 Clerkenwell Green, London, EC 4, England.

William Korn, Inc., 260 West Street, New York 13, New York.

Alfred Metzger, 30 Irving Place, New York 3, New York.

Frank Mittermeier, 3577 East Tremont Avenue, New York 65, New York.

Edward C. Muller, 61-63 Frankfort Street, New York 7, New York.

Nelson-Whitehead Paper Corp., 7 Laight Street, New York 13, New York.

Rembrandt Graphic Arts Co., Inc., Stockton, New Jersey.

Schmidt Lithograph Co., 461-499 Second Street, San Francisco 7, California.

Sleight & Hellmuth, Printing Ink Division, 900 S. Clinton, Chicago, Illinois.

Sun Chemical Corporation, 750 Third Avenue, New York 17, New York.

INDEX